BLOCKCHAIN & CRYPTOCURRENCIES

Lessons from a crypto convert

ANTONIO LUIS LARA

© 2020, Antonio Luis Lara Acedo

SAFE CREATIVE: 2101086527424

The total or partial reproduction of the content (texts and information) of the book, by any means or electronic or mechanical procedure, computer processing, or any other form of transfer of life and work of the author without prior authorization of the copyright holder, is strictly prohibited within limits established by national and international laws, under the maximum penalties provided by law.

To my beloved brother

Disclaimer: This book references an option and is for information purposes only. It is not intended to be investment advice. Seek a duly licensed professional for investment advice.

Index

Index 5
Prolog 7
August 15th, 1971. The day of the Doom 13
SECTION I: BITCOIN & BLOCKCHAIN 20
Chapter 1: The foundations: decentralization and cryptography 21
Chapter 2: Bitcoin genesis 30
Chapter 3: Blockchain 38
Chapter 4: Understanding Bitcoin 49
Chapter 5: Mining. Is it worth it? 56
SECTION II: ETH AND OTHER ALTCOINS. TOKENIZATION 68
Chapter 6: Ethereum genesis 69
Chapter 7: Understanding Ethereum 74
Chapter 8: Smart contracts and DAO 81
Chapter 9: Tokenization 88
Chapter 10: GeoDB 95
Chapter 11: Altcoins 105
SECTION III: INVESTMENT 124
Chapter 12: Decentralized Finance 125
Chapter 13: Real cases 154
Chapter 14: Taxation 180
Chapter 15: Scams 186
Conclusions 191

Acronyms Glossary i
Figure index.. vi
Acknowledgments... viii
About the author ix

Prolog

Better late

    I am a telecommunications technical engineer and a database consultant. I have a postgraduate degree in telematics and telecommunications networks and an MBA. The first time I heard about Bitcoin, I was just out of University. I was young and working in an American technology consulting firm. I had the perfect profile to be one of the first buyers of the new cryptocurrency, except for one thing: I was not passionate about technology. I didn't care. For me, it was just a working tool. What I liked was analyzing and solving problems. When you work as a developer, you use a language, and your mission is to use it in the most appropriate way to obtain an effective and efficient solution to the problem because resources are always limited. My lack of passion at that time is not difficult to understand. Not too many people are enthusiastic about studying Grammar, but thanks to it, you can make great speeches, make someone fall in love, enjoy a chat with friends or write Hamlet. I wouldn't say I like languages either, but I have no choice but to speak English at work and German in everyday life.

That way of thinking made me make one of the most foolish mistakes of my whole life: thinking that the new Bitcoin was a geek's thing. "*Other freaks from a faculty that have nothing else to do but invent a cryptocoin.*" That was my thought.

In time I didn't change my mind either, even though the project got good shape and the coin skyrocketed. In April 2010, the price was 0.3 cents. In July of the same year it reached 8 cents, however, at the end of the year the price reached $13.

Meanwhile, I still thought that, without the support of any state, or any federal reserve, or even an asset, there was no point in investing in it, mostly when volatility was rampant.

My evolution in my workplace didn't help me change my mind, either. As a database developer, I was becoming less and less interested in programming syntax. I stopped worrying about it because it didn't add any value to me. Everything was there, on the Internet. What was important to me was the background, the database engine whose fair use determines the performance, and of course, the business. Business knowledge is everything, or almost.

From my perspective, technology was only the outer layer essential to solve problems, but business knowledge... That's where the real value lies. Without it, technology was like a spoon on an empty plate.

I changed city, country, language: Spanish, Catalan, French, English, German... The language didn't matter. If you had something important to say, someone came and translated it for you. It was the external layer, like programming, like technology.

July 2019. The bitcoin price was around $9,000 after reaching $16,000 in December 2017. In 2019, focused on my true passion, investment, I bought a few GeoDB shares, a new British company with Spanish capital (human and monetary). Their first project was focused on creating a marketplace where companies could acquire anonymous user data, which was (and is) rewarded through a mobile app. The compensation is granted with tokens, a cryptoasset type.

My first contact with the Blockchain came. I thought the idea was interesting, so I started to study the subject: First Bitcoin and Blockchain and then ETH and smart contracts. Suddenly, a new world opened up before my eyes. For the first time for me, technology was not just a problem-solving tool. It was the core, the business, even beyond: the philosophy—the critical piece of a new economic theory with basis on the 19th century and born in the 21st.

I discovered the most crucial technological disruption since the Internet emergence. A change of economic paradigm that, sooner or later, will have to be accepted because of its multiple advantages, the main one being decentralization. It is the most critical Blockchain concept, making it the most democratic solution to current problems and frees cryptocurrencies from state interventions. The third parties needed today to certify payments will tend to disappear. No one will need a bank, Visa, or MasterCard to certify a transfer from a credit card, and it will also be safer and much cheaper.

The Blockchain's dimension is even more significant because it is not only applied to cryptocurrencies, but it goes much further because, as the technology that it is, it still retains its part of "tool" to solve problems.

As immutable chains, the blockchains will serve to eliminate any money laundering. Every movement is stored in the blockchain and cannot be destroyed or modified.

It will reinforce security, preventing digital impersonation of users.

Traceability will be infallible and immutable. Supply chains such as food, medicine, and legal evidence chains will be 100% secure and with a ridiculous maintenance cost.

Any type of registration will be absorbed by this technology, lowering legal, notary, property, vehicle, or intellectual registration costs. Furthermore, after the Ethereums's arrival, the sky is the limit. Thanks to the smart contracts, a programming layer is placed over the blockchain, making it possible for an application such as GeoCash, from GeoDB, to reward users with tokens in exchange for their anonymous data. It is a paradigm shift by which they become beneficiaries of the Big Data business by being rewarded for what they have already done for a long time without any benefits in return. In this case, the contract sends a cryptocurrency payment when a user has transferred a specific amount of data. That can be extrapolated to the purchase of real estate or any commercial transaction. Suddenly the figure of the intermediary disappears. The trustworthy deposit will no longer reside in a third party. It will be located in the network, in the blockchain.

It has taken me 12 years to be convinced of the usefulness of blockchains. I focused on the cryptocurrency and did not see the Blockchain. The wood didn't let me see the trees. Today, I collaborate with GeoDB, and the price of the bitcoin is over $30,000.

Now I am convinced, and I am preparing you to be confident and take advantage of this knowledge for your benefit.

This book is aimed at a broad audience. It would not make sense to dedicate it only to readers with advanced knowledge because the objective is to make everyone participate in the most significant technological revolution of the century, and those already do.

Since the Blockchain goes beyond the purely technological, the first chapter describes the background that explains this disruption's arrival. In the eternal struggle between Keynesians and Liberals, the latter take advantage. Liberal thought, mistreated by some media, finds in the Blockchain an unexpected impulse that will help expand its economic theory. You will see how liberalism, so abused by many in these times, is not synonymous with savage capitalism.

After the first chapter begins a section dedicated to blockchains and Bitcoin and its background, the last chapter of that section is dedicated to mining, the different available and practical examples to see if it is advantageous or not general public.

The second section focuses on ETH, a bitcoin alternative cryptoasset that is the second-largest capitalization. It allows the use of smart contracts and tokens generation based on it. It is worth mentioning a chapter dedicated exclusively to GeoDB as an example of what can be achieved with smart contracts.

The third and last section is dedicated to investment in cryptoassets, the definition of the most critical concepts of decentralized finance, and how to obtain a return from them and their taxation. A short chapter is included with tips to identify and avoid scams, scammers, and other dangers for you and your money.

While this last section can be read without having done the same with the first two, it is highly recommended that it be done sequentially.

I hope you enjoy the book and ride the disruption wave to change the financial system for years to come radically.

August 15th, 1971. The day of the Doom

When a crisis is an opportunity

This book's subject is nowhere near economic theory, nor does it attempt to trace events beyond the last ten years, but only through an understanding of the economic background and global financial reality can the emergence of Blockchain's disruptive technology be understood. It was born because it was necessary.

Some people believe that a currency's value depends on the amount of gold available in the country that puts it into circulation. In other words, the amount of money circulating is directly related to the gold reserves of that state. That relationship no longer exists as it is today.

In 1819, during the Napoleonic Wars, the British Parliament passed the Resumption Act, which returned to establish a fixed price exchange of gold for paper money. This system put an end to using the bimetal standard (gold/silver) due to the difficulty of maintaining the two metals' value at a certain level.

The pillars of the gold standard were as follows:

- The exchange of coins for gold was accepted.
- Free export/import of gold was allowed.
- The value of the national currency unit was equivalent to a certain amount of gold.
- Central bank reserves were constituted in gold to maintain parity between currency and gold.

With their imperfections due to violations of the central banks' rules, these four pillars allowed the exchange of currency at fixed rates, contributed to price stabilization, and avoided large imbalances in the balance of payments.

Portugal adopted the gold standard in 1854, Germany in 1871, and the United States in 1879.

This standard was used in some of its forms by the major world powers in an era of unprecedented prosperity, when the First Industrial Revolution took place and until the outbreak of the first of the great crises that would determine and influence economic thinking during the 20th century: the First World War. The warring countries in the conflict saw their financing needs rise to levels that could not be guaranteed by the gold in their reserves, which led these states to print money without being backed by gold. The only guarantee was the promise of payment by the issuing state. That was the arrival of fiat money.

Naturally, when a weapon of this caliber falls into politicians' hands, nothing good is about to come. The abuse of issuing money without a guarantee on any precious metal resulted in hyperinflation situations like the one experienced in the Weimar Republic between 1921 and 1923. The abuse of issuing paper money without backing led to the cost of living being multiplied by more than two million. Inflation reached the chilling figure of 1,000,000,000,000%.

Figure I.1 Children are playing with Deutsche Marks during hyperinflation

That economic disaster was one of the causes of the rise of the Nazi Party to power in Germany in the 1930s and, therefore, World War II. I hope no one will be surprised that the Teutonic country has since become one of the champions of economic orthodoxy.

Although the Weimar Republic's case is the best known, the record for inflation is held by Hungary, when in 1946 it reached 49.1 trillion percent.

During the rales of the Second World War, representatives from 44 countries met in Bretton Woods, United States, intending to establish a new economic order that would not fall into the same errors of the agreements agreed in the previous war that, among others, favored German hyperinflation. In that convention, one of the most important in history from the economic point of view, not only was the gold standard adopted, but the United States committed to sustain the price of the golden metal at 35 dollars per ounce, eliminating any restriction on the exchange for dollars at that price. In this way, the dollar was established as the international reference currency. Upon creating the World Bank, the International Monetary Fund and the World Trade Organization germ were agreed.

Figure I.2 President Richard Nixon

After a few years of good functioning of that system, in the 60s, due to the Vietnam War, the USA started to print vast amounts of money, and the dollar began to depreciate. For the first time in the 20th century, in 1971, they had a negative trade deficit. Fort Knox's gold reserves contracted, and there was an unprecedented flight of capital. Faced with this situation, on August 15th, 1971, President Richard Nixon decided to violate the Bretton Woods agreements and devaluated the dollar by 10%, in addition to suspending convertibility into gold. He applied a 10% tariff on imports, which forced other nations to revalue their currencies. The gold standard was dead.

In this way, whether he wanted it or not, Nixon laid the foundation for the following economic crises: he laid the foundation for public debt by expanding the money supply.

Since that time, states could issue money without any collateral backup. A dangerous weapon of public spending in the hands of politicians who focus on the short term rather than the long term. With each new issue of money, new debt is generated (generally adopted by external creditors), interest rates become higher and higher. With each additional issue, the risk of default increases, and, worse, the money already circulating in the market depreciates. The ordinary citizen is impoverished to increase public spending, generally in an unproductive way, to enrich a few who will be in charge of developing and implementing these measures. Besides, potential beneficiaries will have to face future interest payments generated by the debt and the devaluation of their savings.

All of the above does not seem like a profitable business. Not at least for the average citizen. But these Keynesian policies are good for politicians who maintain government responsibilities because that offers them short-term liquidity, fundamental for their electoral promises, which impoverishes the citizen in the long term when they will no longer have to hold account for it.

Since then, some think that returning to the gold standard would be the best option, but it would also present fundamental problems:

- Logistics: derivatives of the export, transport, and storage of gold
- Short-term price instability due to deflation caused by improvements in production and inflation from factors such as the discovery of gold mines.

Liberal economists like Hayek or Mises theorized about what should be a currency that would really help the citizen and, therefore, the economy. Mises rightly defended in 1971 in "*The theory of money and credit*," with its principle of solid money, that a currency is solid when the market freely chooses it and is unaware of the negative effect of state obstruction.

Hayek, for his part, in 1989, stated: "*I don't think we will ever have a good currency again before we take it out of the hands of the government, that is to say, we cannot take it out of them with violence, the only thing we can do is to introduce something in a devious and indirect way that cannot stop it.*"

Well, it is already difficult for a currency to be chosen by the market without pressure from the state but, even in that case, we find the problem of trust by which an intermediary is needed in a financial transaction: the problem of double-spending that makes necessary the presence of a third party (usually a bank, Visa, MasterCard, etc.) to prevent the payer from using the same money for more than one transaction. Hence, the coins given to one person will not be the same as those given to another.

Thus, immersed in that system came the year 2008, when the subprime mortgages and Lehman Brothers crash occurred. Once again, a considerable crisis arises that leads to unemployment at unsuspected rates, ruins millions of families, and closes countless businesses. As in previous crises, the breeding ground for extremism and populism was created. Discontent with their leaders and with the financial system grew again among the people.

Amid all this detachment, there is an entity, a person, a group (nobody knows what or who it is) called Satoshi Nakamoto. He was the creator of a paper called "*Bitcoin: A peer-to-peer electronic cash system*." A brief 9-page document that solves the problem of double spending on a secure network that is not (or almost) vulnerable to attacks and proposes a system with a limited number of coins, making Mises and Hayek's dream years ago a reality.

The first Bitcoin block was generated on January 3rd, 2009. That block contained the message "*Chancellor on the brink of second bailout for banks*." A declaration of intent. Bitcoin had come to be an alternative to the international banking and monetary system. That was the beginning of the most disruptive technology since the Internet's appearance.

SECTION I: BITCOIN & BLOCKCHAIN

Chapter 1: The foundations: decentralization and cryptography

> "Dividing or decentralizing power necessarily means reducing the absolute amount of power, and the system of competition is the only system aimed at minimizing, through decentralization, the power that men exercise over men."
>
> Friedrich Hayek, economist and Nobel Prize

It is impossible to understand Blockchain and Bitcoin's concepts without knowing the two fundamental pillars on which they are based: cryptography and decentralization.

Neither of them is a new concept. Both have been used for centuries by humanity. The difference lies in the sophistication that they have been reached in recent years.

The struggle between centralization and decentralization has been a constant for centuries. Even today, there are political debates about it among supporters of a centralist state or one that tends to be federated.

In a centralized system, authority is vested in one person, one entity, or a set of them. The other participants in the system are subordinate to the authority established at a higher level. An individual or group orders, and the rest follow, following a hierarchy or not.

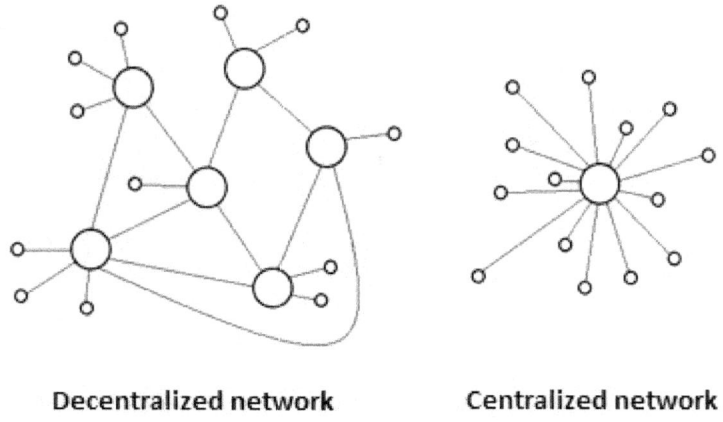

Decentralized network   **Centralized network**

Figure 1.1 Network typologies

In a fully decentralized system, authority is shared among all its members. In the first case, maintaining control is much simpler; however, it has significant drawbacks such as security and lack of democracy. The latter need not be explained, but perhaps the former does. When there is only one leader in the system that sustains control and authority, attacking him and isolating him from the rest, the system is left in a state of chaos and disarray. All relevant information is revealed, and power is lost. A decentralized system is virtually impossible to bring down. To make a decision, and therefore command, one would have to control 51 percent of the individuals who make up the system, being an attack attempt much more difficult. Therefore, every decision will be made by consensus, and there is no room for censorship or relevant information to be controlled by a few. The fact that the info is distributed among all participants means that if someone cheats and tries to change a transaction already made, the rest of the nodes consider it illegitimate and reject it.

In a centralized system, the tolerance to failures is much lower since if the system that controls the rest fails, the system is blocked. That does not happen with decentralization; one node of the network's failure is bearable because the rest will continue to be operational to continue working.

The fact that the system is decentralized entails fundamental problems such as the essential maintenance of trust between participants. But, suppose this problem is solved, what would happen if we had decentralized money?

Put your hand in your pocket, and take out a €10 bill from your wallet. Why does it have that value? It is just a piece of paper with a certain quality and mechanisms that make it difficult to forge. What determines the value is that it has been issued by an entity we all trust: the European Central Bank.

The same happens with monetary transactions. If you buy a TV on Amazon, you pay with a bank card. Both the selling company and the buyer trust that third party to carry out the sale so that it is certified that your money will reach its destination without you being able to use it on another occasion.

Suddenly it is possible to use a currency where the network itself deposits the trust. It is unnecessary to involve a third party that provides trust nor a state that issues it. All transactions will be recorded in the blockchain as if it were a ledger—an immutable account book controlled by all network nodes.

The advantages of decentralized money are clear:

- There is no need for intermediaries, with the noticeable cost reduction that this implies.
- Money is no longer deposited in bank accounts but in a wallet that you own and control.
- Anyone with access to a computer or a cell phone can operate with them.
- The commissions are low since the only thing you pay to make a transfer is the cost of mining, which we will see later.
- The transactions' speed is much higher because the computing is divided, and it is difficult for bottlenecks to occur. That affects the speed perceived by the user.

An exciting concept is that of the DAO (Decentralized Autonomous Organization). It is a type of organization governed by a series of protocols or digital rules, managed in a decentralized way.

After establishing and making public the set of rules that are implemented in a smart contract (it will be explained in detail in chapter 8), funding is requested from the sale of a type of cryptoasset called a token, which can also be used to reward users for carrying out specific activities required by the DAO. Any transaction is recorded in a blockchain and is therefore secure and immutable.

When the organization begins its operation, all management decisions are made by consensus. The main drawback is that any wrong decision made in the initial rules, or even a security problem, cannot be corrected until a majority agreement is reached to establish the change in those rules.

Once the importance of decentralization is understood, it is necessary to know the second pillar on which the blockchains are based: cryptography.

Although it may seem a modern discipline, cryptography has been used for more than 4.000 years. The term, of Greek origin, is composed of *krypto* (hidden) and *graphos* (writing). The purpose that has always been pursued with it is to make a message only interpretable by the origin and the destination so that, if someone intercepts the message, it has no meaning for him. For this reason, it has been systematically used by different armies at different times throughout history. Books such as the *Old Testament* or *The Iliad* refer to ciphers, and both Spartans and Romans used cryptographic methods to encrypt writings. The Caesar cipher, used by the latter, is based on transposition. Each letter of the alphabet had to be changed for a different corresponding one due to advancing the alphabet a fixed number of positions concerning the letter to be encrypted.

From the 9th century onwards, the first "hackers" appeared who, like Al Kindi, author of studies to break the encryption of messages through frequency analysis, contributed to creating more robust algorithms. Thus, in the Renaissance, Leon Alberti created the polyalphabetic cipher to avoid breaking the encryption of messages through frequency analysis.

Possibly, the most famous cases of encryption for military use are the Disk Wheel invented by Thomas Jefferson, third president of the United States, created to encrypt the communications of the rebels in the War of Independence, and the Enigma Machine, made by the German company Scherbius & Ritter. The latter was fundamental in German communications at the beginning of World War II. The breaking of its encryption by an Allied team under Alan Turing's command was decisive for the war.

After the Second World War, the next significant advances in cryptography would come in the 1970s. Those new developments would give way to modern cryptography: encryption with an asymmetric key.

Until that time, all algorithms had used symmetric keys, or in other words, both sender and receiver had to know the key to decrypt the message. However, Whitfield Diffie and Martin Hellman designed a new type of cryptographic algorithm with two keys: a public one used for encryption and a private one for decryption.

Thus, it is necessary to know both keys to access the content of the message.

That encryption system with public key and decryption with private key allows everyone to know who sent the message, but only the legitimate recipient can access its content.

Figure 1.2 Whitfield Diffie and Martin Hellman

In the case of Bitcoin, a variant of asymmetric key cryptography, based on elliptic curves, is used, which utilizes shorter keys while maintaining security at the same level. The public key is employed to receive the transactions since it can be known by everyone, while the private key is used to sign the transactions. It is essential to show that a signature can be validated using the public key without knowing or making visible the private key.

Public key encryption generates a hash code whose purpose is to check the message's integrity received by the receiver. Since a hash function applied to two files creates two different hash codes, the receiver will check whether the message has been modified.

That is one of the Bitcoin mining basics and will be explained in detail in the corresponding chapter.

One of the significant advantages is that at no time is a trusted third party required to create the keys because they are randomly generated.

In short, thanks to cryptography, the immutability of the information and the security of the transactions are guaranteed.

Remember the main points of this chapter:

Blockchain is based on two pillars: cryptography and decentralization.

Decentralized systems are more robust and secure. The fall of one node of the network is bearable because the rest will remain operational to continue working.

There is no need for intermediaries with decentralized money, with the noticeable cost reduction that this implies.

It is not deposited in bank accounts but in a wallet that you own and control.

A DAO (Decentralized Autonomous Organization) is a type of organization directed by a series of protocols that is managed in a decentralized manner.

Thanks to cryptography, the immutability of information and the security of transactions are guaranteed.

Chapter 2: Bitcoin genesis

"When spiders come together, they can tie up a lion."

Ethiopian proverb

In the introduction of this book, the creator of Bitcoin, Satoshi Nakamoto, is mentioned. Behind this pseudonym, there is a person or group of people. Experts like Laszlo Hanyecz, a computer programmer and cybersecurity expert, and the person who paid 10,000 BTC (bitcoins) to purchase two pizzas on May 22nd, 2010, believe that the Bitcoin code is too well developed to have a single creator. Therefore, we would be looking at a project carried out by an anonymous group or institution composed of cryptography experts. In reality, the technological level is so high that it is possible to suspect who was behind the cryptocurrency. In 2008 the number of recognized experts in the cryptographic field was not as high as today.

Although Satoshi Nakamoto (let's talk about him as if he were a person) is the main responsible for the fact that Papa John's Pizza got 10.000 BTC for two pizzas (about 129 million dollars as of November 2020), his work would not be understood without the work of several experts, developed from the 80s of the last century, not to mention that, in turn, they are based on the paper "*New Directions in Cryptography*," by Martin Hellman and Whitfield Diffie in which they defined a new public key cryptographic system back in 1978.

It could be said that the first antecedent of Bitcoin was the proposal of digital money described by David Chaum, from the Department of Computer Science of the University of California, in his article "*Blind Signatures for Untraceable Payments*" published in 1982. He proposed the use of blind signature cryptography to achieve the untraceability of digital money payments.

The blind signature protocol allows an entity to receive a signed message to be presented to a third party without revealing who is sending it.

Figure 2.1 David Chaum

In 1988, already located in Amsterdam, he deepened in this idea and, together with Amos Fiat and Moni Naor, wrote a paper called "*Untraceable Electronic Cash*" and improved its original concept to introduce an offline system transaction that allowed the detection of double-spending. That's the problem by which a digital currency could be spent more than once and which MasterCard or Visa solves when paid by card. These two companies guarantee that the purchase's money goes directly to the seller and no one else.

In 1990 Chaum founded DigiCash, an e-currency company based in Amsterdam that he used as a shuttle for his researches. Four years later, the company made the first electronic payment. In 1999, the company went bankrupt, not for lack of opportunities to keep the business running.

Before the end of DigiCash's operations in 1993, he collaborated with Stefan Brands to create the paper "*Distance bounding protocols,*" through which a distance boundary is established between the parties involved in a transaction.

DigiCash received offers of collaboration from Microsoft, whereby DigiCash would implement the digital money within Windows 95. He had similar offers from Netscape and even Visa, but all of them were declined. Many people think that Chaum lacked entrepreneurial vision; others believe that he had a much more ambitious goal in mind. But that goes into the world of speculation and has never been proven to be directly related to bitcoin, much less to Satoshi Nakamoto.

In 1997, Adam Back developed HashCash, an algorithm to combat spam based on the proof of work, base of the future bitcoin.

The proof of work consisted of solving a very complex cryptographic problem that required the sender's CPU and electricity consumption. This work results in a hash code sent to a server to check it at almost no cost. The entire workload falls on the sender side. Thus, if this "price" is set by sending an email, sending them in bulk would be very expensive for the sender. Interestingly, Adam Back based his work on another developed by Moni Naor, an Israeli computer scientist who collaborated with David Chaum to create his digital money.

Today, the Bitcoin network's miners get their rewards for solving proofs of work based on the HashCash algorithm.

Figure 2.2 Adam Back's Twitter profile

Another predecessor of the current Bitcoin is b-money, created by Wei Dai in 1998. It was intended to be an *"anonymous, decentralized electronic cash system."* Its purpose was to provide many of the services and features that new cryptocurrencies offer today. It was never officially launched, but it laid the foundation for future digital currencies with elements that remain in today's cryptocurrencies, such as the use of proof of work for mining.

In 1998, Nick Szabo proposed a decentralized financial system using common Bitcoin elements, such as timestamped blocks and proof of work protocol. All this in a blockchain called BitGold. As a b-money, it was never released. In fact, Nick Szabo's paper was never officially published. However, in a 2010 article, Satoshi Nakamoto wrote: "*Bitcoin is a proposed implementation of Wei Dai, b-money in Cypherpunks in 1998 and Nick Szabo's BitGold.*"

In 2004, Hal Finney published "*RPOW - Reusable Proof of Work,*" where he proposed a reusable proof of work. Years earlier, he published "*Detecting Double Spend*" and "*Digital Cash and privacy.*"

So decisive were these works that Wei Dai and Nick Szabo, together with Hal Finney, were the first developers Nakamoto turned to develop his project. Hal Finney, in particular, gave enthusiastic support to the project. He downloaded the Bitcoin software on the day of the launch and received the first transaction: 10 BTC from Nakamoto.

Finney, who has been suffering from ALS since August 2009 and died in 2014, is another candidate to play Satoshi Nakamoto's role. He is currently cryopreserved at the Alcor Life Extension Foundation, awaiting treatment for his disease.

In 2010 Nakamoto handed over the project to Gavin Andersen as the lead developer of the Bitcoin Foundation. Currently, the CEO of the foundation is Llew Claasen.

It is important to note that many of the scientists cited in this chapter, led by Chaum, have been part of the cypherpunk movement, aiming to preserve digital users' identity through cryptography.

On the cypherpunk mailing list, the most reputable scientists were publicizing their work and sharing their impressions. It was also the place where the Cryptoanarchist Manifesto and the Cyphernomicon were created.

Some of the essential points of the Cryptoanarchist Manifesto are summarized in the following lines:

"Privacy in an open society also requires cryptography. If I say something, I want that to be heard only by those I intend to hear. If the content of my speech is available to everyone, I have no privacy. To encrypt or cipher is to indicate the desire for privacy, so to encrypt or cipher with weak cryptography is to indicate that my desire for privacy is not as great."

"We cypherpunks are dedicated to building anonymous systems. We are defending our privacy with cryptography, anonymous mail systems, digital signatures, and electronic money.

"Privacy is a necessity for achieving an open society in the electronic age. Privacy is not the same as secrecy. You don't want everyone to know a private matter, but a secret matter is something you don't want anyone to know. Privacy is the power to choose to reveal yourself to the world when you choose to do so."

"The traditional banking model achieves a level of privacy by limiting access to information to the parties involved and a trusted third party. The need to publicly announce all transactions rules out this method, but privacy can still be maintained by breaking the flow of information elsewhere: by keeping public keys anonymous. The public can see that someone is sending an amount to someone else, but without the information that ties the transaction to a person. That is similar to the level of information published by currency exchange centers, where the time and amount of individual exchanges is made known without mentioning the parties involved."

The members of this movement put their philosophy into practice and ultimately led to the creation of Bitcoin.

Remember the main points of this chapter:

> Satoshi Nakamoto was the creator of Bitcoin, but he relied on the work of great cryptography experts.
>
> Coins like DigiCash, b-coin, and BitGold are considered the predecessors of today's Bitcoin.
>
> Adam Back developed in 1997 an algorithm to combat spam based on the proof of work, the basis of Bitcoin.
>
> The calculation of the hash code is costly, but checking if it's correct doesn't take up much of your resources
>
> Since the end of the last century, many of the most important cryptographic experts have been part of the cypherpunk movement, aiming to preserve digital users' identity through cryptography.

Chapter 3: Blockchain

> "Whereas most technologies tend to automate workers on the periphery doing menial tasks, blockchains automate away the center. Instead of putting the taxi driver out of a job, blockchain puts Uber out of a job and lets the taxi drivers directly work with the customer.
>
> Vitálik Buterin, developer and Ethereum cofounder

Once the background and historical context are known, it is time to get down to the core, and nothing better than starting with Blockchain, the foundation on which the rest of the book is based.

A blockchain is a digital data structure shared in a decentralized way among all network nodes. It is characteristic that once a transaction is performed (and verified), it cannot be modified. From that moment, all the nodes of the network have a copy of the transaction. In this way, hacking it would imply doing the same in 51% of the nodes so that the rest would consider the modification as correct. That is almost impossible in practice.

But how does this whole process work?

All transactions must be hosted in fixed-size blocks that are linked together. The miners are in charge of this task, and they get a reward for their computational effort. Ideally, a block should be completed to its maximum size, but this does not always happen.

Each transaction includes a timestamp (information about the exact time the operation was performed), information about the source and destination, and a hash code created from the current transaction's content and the hash of the previous transaction.

In a blockchain, not all the nodes are the same, but there are four types with specific functionalities:

- Full node: These are nodes that store the complete blockchain.
- Router node: Their primary mission is to make routing functions, although they can store the blockchain.
- Client node: They are nodes that allow users to check if their transaction has been carried out correctly, quickly, and straightforwardly.
- Miners: They are the mining nodes that are in charge of calculating the hash code.

Below is an example of block creation that is very simplified and therefore not entirely accurate but will help you understand this technology's basics.

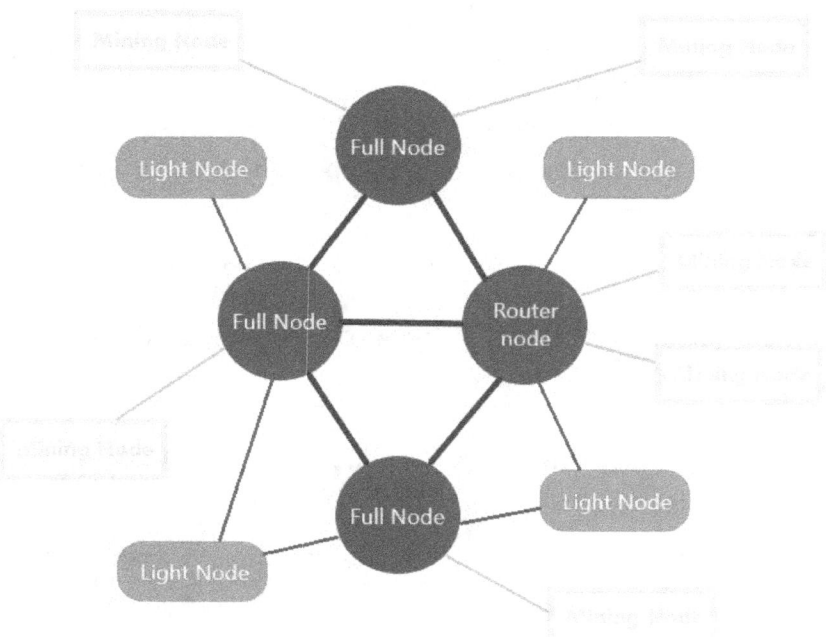

Figure 3.1 Node distribution in a blockchain

It is much simpler when explained with an example: Let's suppose that five friends (Anthony, Frank, Mariah, Lisa, and James) have decided to live together and need to keep track of the money each one spends on household expenses and loans made to each other. They need an incorruptible system, and that does not need a third person to validate the operations. For simplicity's sake, let's assume that a block contains a single transaction. They use a hash function to create a code that uniquely identifies each transaction. Besides, the hash function has the peculiarity that calculating the code for a block's content is difficult, but checking that it is valid is a quick and easy task.

The blockchain starts when Anthony lends five euros to James, creating a transaction including the sender, the receiver, the amount, a unique id, and the fees, among others:

The transaction is sent to the network to which Anthony and James belong until it can be included in a block by the miners. Then, they try to calculate the hash for the block. The first node that gets the hash code sends it to the rest, who check if the hash is correct. This protocol is called Proof of Work (PoW) and is used to validate and chain the transactions and reward the miners. In this way, consensus is reached between nodes, the block remains as it appears in the following image, and the miner who generated the hash gets a reward. As it is the first block, the hash of the previous block is not included.

block number	1
timestamp	11/11/2020 09:56:25.251
sender	Anthony
receiver	James
amount	5 euros
last block hash	
hash	0x123123ADE3400

The next transaction occurs when Mariah does her weekly shopping at a supermarket:

block number	2
timestamp	11/11/2020 10:03:55.003
sender	Mariah
receiver	Supermarket
amount	150 euros
last block hash	0x123123ADE3400
hash	

Again, it reaches the miners. The fasted one obtains the hash code (which is calculated with the content of the current transaction and the hash of the previous one) gets the reward after the other nodes accept the result.

Now the blockchain looks like this:

block number	1
timestamp	11/11/2020 09:56:25.251
sender	Anthony
receiver	James
amount	5 euros
last block hash	
hash	0x123123ADE3400

block number	2
timestamp	11/11/2020 10:03:55.003
sender	Mariah
receiver	Supermarket
amount	150 euros
last block hash	0x123123ADE3400
hash	0x1E5173ADE7900

All participants in the network receive the complete blockchain.

Finally, Lisa invites Frank to dinner at a restaurant. The process is repeated, and the blockchain is as follows:

block number	1
timestamp	11/11/2020 09:56:25.251
sender	Anthony
receiver	James
amount	5 euros
last block hash	
hash	0x123123ADE3400

block number	2
timestamp	11/11/2020 10:03:55.003
sender	Mariah
receiver	Supermarket
amount	150 euros
last block hash	0x123123ADE3400
hash	0x1E5173ADE7900

block number	3
timestamp	11/11/2020 21:27:06.041
sender	Lisa
receiver	Restaurant
amount	80 euros
last block hash	0x1E5173ADE7900
hash	0x23CBA328A1C00

Remember that this whole chain is replicated in all the nodes of the network.

If James now decided to hack the chain to modify Anthony's loan, it would be complicated.

First, he would have to access the initial block, make the modification and calculate the hash code, which is a task that consumes a lot of resources, but he would also have to modify the hash codes of all the subsequent transactions. That may not seem very complicated with only three transactions, but you must think that there are millions of transactions in a blockchain so that the computation time would be very high. From time to time, the hash calculation complexity increases, and the reward obtained for it decreases to cope with computer equipment's computational improvements. It becomes increasingly difficult to carry out an attack.

But even if he had achieved all of the above, He would not have achieved anything either. The rest of the nodes have the original copy of the blockchain that has not been altered. To make the change, he would have to convince 51% of the participating nodes to accept the change. We come back to the same thing, in a blockchain, thousands of nodes participate, so the mission becomes impossible. Eliminating or modifying a transaction would imply such a high cost that, at present, it is unfeasible.

Note that in the above example, PoW has been used as a consensus protocol. Bitcoin uses this protocol, but there are many others with their advantages and disadvantages. The most important ones are as follows:

Proof of Work (PoW)

It is the most famous consensus protocol. It's used in Bitcoin and was developed by Adam Back, as we saw in chapter 2. The nodes focus all their computational effort on solving a cryptographic problem and adding the hash to the string. Their main problem is the high consumption of resources.

Reusable Proof of Work (RPoW)

As mentioned at the time, RPoW is a PoW algorithm created by Hall Finney based on Adam Back's HashCash.

In this case, the PoW in the form of a token can be changed to one that allows it to be sent to another server requiring a PoW. In this way, the work of the servers is reduced.

Proof of Stake (PoS)

It is one of the main alternatives to PoW. Instead of consuming resources (the miner with more resources has more chance to solve the problem), the miners buy tokens. The miner with the most tokens can validate the block and thus receive the reward. In short, money calls to money or tokens call to tokens. That is the consensus protocol used in the second version of the Ethereum.

Proof of Elapsed Time (PoET)

It is an algorithm designed for private blockchains and not for cryptocurrencies. It makes it much easier to scale the network. It is the right solution for logistic processes with a lot of traffic in which it is necessary to maintain traceability without any problem.

There is a controller that randomly selects the nodes to perform the validation. Once the controller receives the cryptographic operation from the selected node, it validates it and adds it to the blockchain.

It is necessary to have an Intel processor to participate in block generation since this is the only processor that can generate the necessary type of random number accepted by the system.

Proof of Importance (PoI)

The validation will fall on the node that performs more transactions and make the calculations faster. Those will do the work and get the reward.

In the previous paragraphs, mention is made of the existence of public and private blockchains that, together with the hybrid ones, make up the three types of blockchains that exist today:

Public Blockchain

These are the ones that can be accessed by anyone with an internet connection. Bitcoin and Ethereum are their two leading exponents.

Private Blockchain

Since the Bitcoin's arrival, many companies and institutions have become interested in blockchains' operations and created their own with their particularities and accessible only to their members.

Generally, they are not decentralized, although they are distributed. There is a central control authority that allows access to users.

Hybrid Blockchain

It is a type of Blockchain mixed with the two previous ones. They are ideal for maintaining the traceability and security in some private elements that should not be modified but can be accessed by an extensive public. Access to the network is controlled, but reading the network content can be extended to a group of people or even to every user with an Internet connection.

After knowing what the blockchains offer us, it is easy to guess that it is not only applicable to the field of cryptocoins but that it could be done to many of them, especially those for which traceability and security is an indispensable requirement. Thus, we will see it implemented in production chains, logistics systems, health records, and food and medicine traceability chains in the near future. It will also boost the development of the Internet of Things. Any device can be connected to the Internet, and the need for security, traceability, immutability, and fault tolerance must be taken to the extreme.

Remember the main points of this chapter:

> A blockchain is a digital data structure shared in a decentralized way between all nodes in a network.
>
> Once a transaction is performed (and verified), it is stored in a block and cannot be modified.
>
> When the block is validated, it is added to the chain.
>
> There are three types of nodes: full, light and miner.
>
> All the nodes in the network (except the light nodes) have a copy of the entire blockchain from the blockchain's beginning.
>
> All miner nodes compete to calculate a hash code that will determine if the block is valid.
>
> The calculation of the hash code is very complex and consumes a lot of resources. That's why the miner who solved it is rewarded.
>
> The protocols by which all the nodes compete to find the solution are called consensus protocols.

Chapter 4: Understanding Bitcoin

> "Bitcoin is the beginning of something great: a currency without a government, something necessary and imperative."
>
> Nassim Taleb, mathematical statistician and writer

The main problem of capitalism is that, sometimes, the interests of the different stakeholders involved in a system are opposed.

Let's take as an example: a company that manufactures and sells mobile phones. The system's stakeholders in which this company works are its workers, customers, suppliers, board of directors, and shareholders. The company's ultimate goal is to generate profits for its owners, for which it needs to sell a product with a reasonable quality/price ratio to its customers. As everybody knows, customers want to buy at the lowest possible price, which implies downward pressure on the professionals who manufacture the product and the suppliers' prices. It is also not uncommon for the board of directors' primary objective to get their bonuses and maintain their power level. That need not necessarily be linked to a higher return for the shareholder.

Bitcoin is a blockchain that, in addition to eliminating that problem at a single stroke, allows us not to depend on third parties (whether a bank, Visa, MasterCard, or PayPal) to certify a cryptocurrency transaction. All participating parties benefit. It's a win to win.

You or I, as users, use this cryptocurrency either as a haven, as a long term investment, or as a speculative investment. In either case, what we need is a fast, secure network with low transaction costs. The more transactions are made, the more miners are rewarded for their computing effort, and there is no downward pressure from users to make a miner's profitless.

The necessary infrastructure is available thanks to the nodes, which can validate a block, store and save the blockchain, and send the information to the rest of the nodes to update the whole system.

There are the following types of nodes in Bitcoin:

Full nodes and supernodes

They form the core of the network. Each block is checked and stored in them. Therefore, in each node of these types, the whole chain is stored from the first block to the last. They are in charge of the verification and are essential in the consensus mechanism. They also perform routing tasks by directing the strings to other nodes.

Lightweight nodes or SPV (Simple Payment Verification)

They connect to complete nodes or supernodes. Their purpose is to check if a transaction has been carried out correctly in a fast and straightforward way. They require few resources to operate.

Miners nodes

They group transactions and encapsulate them in blocks. Once the block is complete, it is sent to the network for validation. Due to the high cost of creating the block, these nodes receive rewards in bitcoin and a commission.

All these nodes live in a decentralized network where decisions are made by consensus, working on open source, which means that anyone can change the code and improve it to bring more speed or security. That new code will only be imposed on the old one if most network nodes find it convenient. That gives the nodes a great deal of autonomy and, therefore, the power to introduce undesired behavior into a money transaction.

Of course, all of the above adds a degree of uncertainty that makes it necessary for a reliable third party to certify that a transaction has been done correctly and that sender and receiver are who they say they are.

But how has Bitcoin managed to eliminate the need for an intermediary to attest that a transaction has been done correctly?

The solution to transmitting information safely in a hostile environment has been studied and resolved long before Bitcoin appeared. This security problem, associated with distributed systems, is known as the **Byzantine Generals Problem**. This dilemma tries to solve the transmission of a message between two or more elements through an unreliable system in which the information can be altered. A group of Byzantine generals are entrenched around a besieged city they intend to conquer. The generals, camped in remote locations within the encirclement, must study and agree on an attack plan. They use messengers who send their different opinions about how best to achieve the objective. Also, there may be some traitor that could send wrong information about the enemy among the generals. The solution to this problem is to find an algorithm that allows all loyal generals to agree on a plan of attack and not be interfered with by traitors' plans.

Bitcoin solves this problem with the PoW algorithm mentioned in the previous chapter.

In this case, the loyal generals (the legitimate nodes) intend to decide whether a transaction is valid or not, and the traitorous nodes can't influence them.

The algorithm bases its strength on mining. The nodes of the network are prepared to solve a mathematical problem created with a hash function. It is very complex and takes a long time to compute. Besides, it includes a timestamp with the time of the transaction. Since there is a considerable expenditure of resources, the node that manages to solve it will reward bitcoin and a small commission.

All mining nodes connected to the network work in unison to solve the problem until one of them finds the solution. The complexity is so high that a mining time of 10 minutes is estimated, after which a new block of 1 MB is created, including the confirmed transactions. It is then sent to the rest of the nodes (complete nodes or supernodes) to verify it. This verification on the other nodes is fast. If the calculations are correct, then the network checks that it is not a double expense. If the solution is wrong or a double expense, access to the network is prevented, and the chain is rejected. Suppose the solution is correct, and it is not a question of a double expenditure. In that case, the information is validated and stored. Network access is given to forward the information, and the miner is rewarded.

Since the nodes' computing capacity is increased over time, thanks to technological improvements, every 2,100 blocks, a recalculation of the mining capacity is performed, increasing the problem's complexity to be solved if necessary. In this way, it is guaranteed that the mining time remains stable.

Therefore, the problem's resolution must be costly in computing time, but verification is immediate.

This consensus algorithm makes Bitcoin vulnerable to the 51% attack, but it's not feasible, as explained above. There are currently more than 10,000 complete nodes in the Bitcoin network. To carry out this attack, the hacker would need to control at least

5,100. He'd also need to have a good number of mining nodes with very high computing power to create the block. If this already has a high cost, the Blockchain protocol itself would also raise computing cost, so it is unfeasible (at least until the popularization of quantum computers).

An interesting term that has not been discussed so far is *halving*. It could be defined as an automatic mechanism to reduce by half the rewards for the mining of bitcoins, which occurs every 210,000 blocks.

In the beginning, Satoshi Nakamoto established a maximum limit of 21 million bitcoins that would be released as transactions were made and the miners worked.

At first, the reward for mining a block (which could be done with a regular PC) was 50 BTC. Today, high computing power is needed to create that same block, and the reward is 6.25 BTC.

This technique ensures that as long as the bitcoin values are small, the reward is high, whereas with the growth of the network and the number of blocks (which implies more demand and higher price), the bitcoin values will be high, and therefore the reward in BTC is smaller.

Once the 21 million bitcoins have been reached, the miners will only be rewarded with commissions.

One of Nakamoto's initial goals was to contain inflation. The fact of accumulating BTC while waiting for it to continue rising, due to the demand increasing and supply decreasing because of halvings, contributes to savings and, therefore, to containing inflation.

Remember the main points of this chapter:

> Bitcoin is a vast open-source database that stores a chain of blocks in a decentralized way and makes decisions by consensus.
>
> There are four types of nodes: Supernodes, complete, SPV, and miners.
>
> It solves the problem of Byzantine generals with the PoW protocol.
>
> Bitcoin miners compete with each other to solve a cryptographic problem that takes about ten minutes to solve. The node that solves it receives a reward.
>
> Each new block includes all new transactions that have been confirmed since the last mining. Its size is one Megabyte.
>
> The mining node that solves the problem sends the new block to the rest of the nodes for validation. If it is verified as correct, it is stored and forwarded throughout the network. If it is incorrect, it is rejected.
>
> Every 2,100 blocks, a recalculation of the network computation capacity is performed to increase the mining complexity if necessary.
>
> Every 210,000 blocks, there is a reduction in the reward given to miners.

The total supply of Bitcoin will be 21 million when the last mining is done.

Chapter 5: Mining. Is it worth it?

"If you don't find a way to make money while you sleep, you will work until you die."

Warren Buffett, economist and investor

In the previous chapter, the concept of mining was introduced. By now, it is clear to us that:

- Mining is the work that all mining nodes do to solve a complex mathematical puzzle, which is broadcast on the network every 10 minutes, which is about the time it takes to solve.
- Of all the nodes, the one who solves the problem correctly (and is validated by the complete nodes) will get the reward.
- Mining involves a high computational effort and expenditure of energy resources.
- Every 210,000 blocks, the reward is reduced to half. It is currently at 6.25 BTC per block mined.
- Every 2,100 blocks, the network's computational capacity is recalculated to adapt the problem's complexity to the new reality.

- It is increasingly complex to mine a block, and the amount of bitcoins received is lower.

After all these statements, some questions must be asked: but how is this done? Is the PC at home worth it? Are there other alternatives? Is it really worth it? Will I be wasting electricity?

This chapter will answer all these questions and present calculators that make it easier to get that answer.

To mine bitcoins, we must first get a mining node. There are two possibilities for that: buying or renting HW. Besides, once you have decided on one of these options, you can choose to participate in a mining pool or not. Let's see case by case.

HW PURCHASE

Until 2013 it was possible to mine BTC with a home computer with a good CPU and a powerful graphics card or with an FPGA (Field Programmable Gate Array). The latter are small devices with a reprogrammable architecture, which is a not inconsiderable advantage. It implies that they can be optimized and oriented to a specific purpose (in this case, the BTC mining). They are cheap and low consumption devices. They make it possible to create a farm at a reasonable price, and, best of all, they can be "reinvented." If a computer's features aren't enough to mine Bitcoin after a while, it could be reprogramed to mine another cryptocurrency that needs fewer resources. These devices are usually programmed in VHDL or Verilog.

The most used FPGAs are the Xilinx Spartan series. They are devices of an adequate power that can work parallel with other units, thus multiplying their computing capacity. They offer a performance of up to 1.25 GB/s and can be purchased for about $135 per unit.

Even today, they are used for small-scale mining, especially for other cryptosystems than Bitcoin.

ASICs have been available since 2013, and today they are the minimum you can own to carry out this work with bitcoin.

An ASIC (Application-Specific Integrated Circuit) is a device with a set of processors designed and optimized specifically for a particular purpose, in this case, the mining of Bitcoin, but also exist for mining other cryptocurrencies such as ETH and other applications not related to crypto at all.

Unlike FPGAs, they are designed for a specific purpose and are not reprogrammable, so once they become obsolete, it won't be easy to give them any use.

They are expensive devices that are difficult to find in the market. They have a very, very high energy consumption and need expensive cooling equipment. Along with the problem of electricity consumption, the main disadvantage is that the obsolescence of these products is very high since it is necessary to maintain a higher computing capacity than the rest of the nodes to successfully mine and depends much on technological advances in the HW, which as we all know are quite fast.

There are big brands that produce quality ASICs. The most recognized ones are Canaan, which is cheaper and has a high power, and Bitmain, which controls 90% of these devices' sales, and the most giant mining farms in the world located in China and Russia.

The following are the characteristics of two of the most sold ASICs:

Canaan Avalon 1047 37 TH/s Bitcoin Miner

- Medium range.
- Hashrate: 37 TH/s.
- Energy consumption: 2,380 W -5 %...+8 %.
- Air cooling.
- Price: $600.

Bitmain Antminer S19 95 TH Bitcoin Miner

- High range.
- Hashrate: 95 TH/s.
- Energy consumption: 3,250 W -10 % ...+10 %.
- Air cooling.
- Price: $3,800.

Bitmain Antminer S19 Pro

- High range.
- Hashrate: 110 TH/s.
- Energy consumption: 3,500 W.
- Air cooling.
- Price: $3,500.

The accumulation of mining farms in China and Russia, where very high computing power is concentrated, and electricity prices are low, make mining in this way not worthwhile because, in addition to the high investment in metal (HW), another factor comes into play that is decisive: the price of the KWh.

Let's look at two examples of mining profitability, leaving behind the issue of taxation, to which chapter 14 will be dedicated, using a specific calculator (www.cryptocompare.com) and assuming a price kWh similar to the Spanish case: 0.1 €. Also, participation in a pool is taken for granted (we will talk about this later) with a 1% fee.

In Spain, for a participation with a Bitmain Antminer S19 pro with a hash rate of 110 TH/s with a purchase price of $3,500 (2,900 euros), a monthly return of about 115 euros would be obtained, which is equivalent to 1,380 euros per year. Considering that the profit will be lower year after year because the hash rate will be lower than the rest of the competitors, it would take around three years to recover the investment. That does not seem to be a good alternative.

Let's try it now in a country with a cheaper electricity rate like Mexico, where the price is around $0.08 per kWh. There, the monthly return would amount to $195 per month, or $2,340 per year. In that case, the investment would be recovered before the two years, but it doesn't seem to be worth it either.

However, in China, with an average of $0.04 per kWh, the results are much more attractive: $243 per month with a total of $2,916 per year, covering the investment in only 12 months and having at least another year to continue using the machine. In that last case, it worths studying the possibility of investing in the purchase and contemplating the risks such as the BTC volatility, which can do, as it already happened in April 2020, that before a significant fall in the price of bitcoin, many miners had to turn off their machines.

One country where mining bitcoins is cheap is Venezuela, where electricity is almost free. With the configuration mentioned above, about $4,900 per year could be obtained. Still, the country's corruption makes it unwise to think about it because once a miner registers, there is a high probability that his equipment will be seized.

Fortunately or unfortunately, we do not live in China or Venezuela, so let's move on to the next option.

So far, we have studied the option of buying one device or several and start mining alone, but there is always the possibility of joining a mining pool.

A mining pool is a kind of group of miners who concentrate their efforts to mine blocks, in this case, Bitcoin, using a server to which all miners connect, thus losing its characteristic decentralization. By participating in a pool, it's possible to receive small parts of rewards that would not be possible to obtain outside the pool, increasing the bitcoins received considerably compared to the individual option.

It is necessary to install specific software such as cgminer to participate in a pool, although there are many others. Once installed and configured, the coins will be received at the address indicated.

The largest mining pool in the world today is Antpool, which is controlled by the company China Bitmain, which in turn controls 90% of the ASICs. It has 12 % of the global mining capacity. It is a free service that offers high security and supports bitcoin and other cryptocurrencies.

It offers different methods to obtain profits with fees that are not very high:

- PPS/PPS+: The profits obtained by a user are based on the energy spent by its node. The fee is 2.5%.
- PPLNS: Profits are established based on the average contribution that the user has made to the pool over a period of time. The fee, in this case, is 1% per day.

The option of joining a mining pool is objectively better than mining alone, but even so, the returns obtained may not be sufficient to cover the investment in the necessary HW.

This alternative has two major drawbacks: A minimum of programming and computer network knowledge is required, and, above all, it should not be forgotten that one is dependent on a single server. By giving up decentralization to improve the mining performance, one assumes the risk that the group controlling the pool will be left with everything that is mined. Unfortunately, this has happened more than once.

CLOUD MINING

Given conventional mining characteristics, it seems that it is not the best of the alternatives, but there is an option for those who do not want to invest in complex computer equipment: rental.

For a long time, there have been platforms that rent a percentage of a farm's production capacity and pay the user the same percentage of the profits obtained. Of course, as there is an intermediary, the potential returns are not very high. If someone decides on this type of mining, it is much more advisable to opt for Ethereum or Litecoin, which offer higher profits.

The number of companies offering these services is huge, but only a few are what they say they are. The rest are usually pyramid schemes and Ponzi schemes.

That's why this chapter includes some of the major reliable companies. Another thing is whether the performance they offer is worth it or not.

Genesis Mining

It is the leading and largest cloud mining company, which is a guarantee in terms of security. The customer service is good. It allows the mining of other currencies such as ETH.

Depending on the moment, you can find different offers. Sometimes their stock runs out, and they cannot offer mining in bitcoin or any other currency until they have free capacity.

For bitcoin, they offer contracts based on a single down payment. On the website, there are currently three types with a duration of 18 months:

- Gold: 3 TH/s for $139.
- Platinum: 35 TH/s for $1,544.
- Diamond: 140 TH/s for $5,880.

Also, maintenance fees will be charged on 28% of the bitcoins obtained.

Using a BTC profit calculator, such as the one offered by 99bitcoins.com, it can be seen that, with the most expensive of the contracts, a quantity of bitcoins equivalent to $6,100 per year (at the price of November 2020) would be obtained, which is equivalent to $9,150 at the end of the contract.

Therefore, the expected benefit would be: $9,150 obtained by mining less $5,880 of the contract price less $1,470 of maintenance fees. This way, its investment results in a $1,800, as long as the BTC price remains stable, which is quite unlikely.

If the prices have changed when you go to the website, repeat the calculations made here.

StormGain

It has some advantages, such as an excellent anti-fraud engine, regular payments, and good customer service. The mining is free but at a low speed. It is not offered as a product itself but as an added value for users who already have a trading account. The mining capacity is increased according to the trading account's contributions (from $15 to $15,000 per month). All profits can be withdrawn, but only for trading within the application.

CCG Mining

This platform also allows for the mining of other cryptosystems such as ETH or Litecoin.

It offers contracts from one year with 25 TH/s for $1,991 with a daily commission per TH/s of $0.17, which would be about $1,551 of total commission at the end of the contract.

The estimated profit after one year would be about $1,089, which is clearly a ruinous business.

From the above examples, it is necessary to study the commissions in detail. In the case of Genesis, with another type of contract similar to CCG's but with a fee of $0.15 per TH/s, there would be substantial losses.

By way of conclusion, it can be said that, given the volatility of the bitcoin price, if you are really interested in obtaining profits through bitcoin, you should pay special attention to the third section of this book, dedicated to investment in cryptocurrencies, which will help you obtain profits, in some cases, in double digits with the advantage of having total liquidity in most of the products you can access.

Remember the main points of this chapter:

At present, it is not possible to mine with a PC. It is necessary to buy or rent a specific HW.

The profitability of mining depends on electricity's price, making the investment in most countries not worthwhile.

Participating in a mining pool is usually more profitable than doing it individually. Still, investing in DeFi or cryptoassets is generally more advantageous.

Before making any investment in HW or cloud mining, it is highly recommended to simulate it in any of the calculators included in this chapter.

SECTION II: ETH AND OTHER ALTCOINS. TOKENIZATION

Chapter 6: Ethereum genesis

"It's clear to me now that Ethereum is the new currency of the Internet. It's way ahead of where PayPal was in its day, and it's much more exciting to its customers than PayPal ever was."

Gil Penchina, Wikia former CEO and eBay vice president

Ethereum is the empirical proof that no one knows how far a genius can go with a lot of spare time until you piss him off. It doesn't matter if he is 17.

Vitálik Buterin was a 16-year-old Russian boy who emigrated to Canada at the age of 6. He was an enthusiastic player of World of Warcraft, an online multiplayer role-playing game. Suddenly, and without warning, the video game creators changed the character's features that our teenager used to play. Vitálik spent the whole night crying because of the damned change, and from that moment, he understood how hard life is, or rather, the problems that centralized systems entail. WoW lost a player forever, and the world gained a math virtuous desiring to change the world.

Soon after, Buterin met Bitcoin from his father, a computer scientist by profession. I wasn't the only one who was wrong, he also thought bitcoin had no future as a currency, but the fact that it was out of the clutches of a government or a corporation, was very attractive to him.

Figura 6.1 Vitálik Buterin

Little by little, he was introduced to the Bitcoin world by participating in forums and attending conferences. He even founded Bitcoin Magazine together with Mihai Alisie. In 2013 he left his university studies to participate in projects around Bitcoin. He received a *Thiel Scholarship for Entrepreneurs* who leave the university with the goal of developing a promising project, with an amount of $100,000. At the end of that same year, he already thought that Bitcoin's functionality was short and incomplete, and it was possible to expand its use thanks to a new layer above the protocol to execute code. Suddenly, a simple currency could become something much more alive and complicated, making decisions by itself according to pre-established rules called smart contracts. The use of blockchains for other purposes than facilitating monetary transactions was coming: the token concept was born.

Everything was triggered very quickly after the publication of the white paper "*A Next-Generation Smart Contract & Decentralized Application Platform.*" Together with Gavin Wood and Joseph Lubin, he created the Ethereum project, launching an ICO (Initial Coin Offering) for the first time in history to obtain financing. In July 2015, the Ethereum Frontier network was launched, a kind of test network that allowed developers worldwide to start creating projects based on smart contracts and tokens. In March 2016, Ethereum Homestead was launched as a stable network, and a month later, a milestone was reached that deserves to be engraved with golden letters in business history. The first DAO (Distributed Autonomous Organization) was launched: a fully automated and decentralized management company where decisions are made based on a smart contract. In less than a month, the project had raised $150 million from 11,000 investors

On May 26th, 2016, Dino Mark, Vlad Zamfir, and Emin Gün Sirer published "*A Call for a Temporary Moratorium on The DAO,*" a report warning of vulnerabilities the autonomous organization's code and calling for a moratorium. They had discovered a problem of double-spending that could be exploited by some users. That was the case. On the night of June 17th, 2016, a programmer managed to divert more than 3 million ETH (50 million dollars) to his wallet, a third of the total investment.

Given the magnitude of that disaster, a quick decision had to be taken. It was made, not without controversy, since it violated the very spirit of Ethereum: they would undo the changes in the blockchain, which in theory is immutable, until the day before the attack and pass all the ETH to another DAO. In this way, investors would recover their tokens. However, to carry out this task, it had to be submitted to all network participants' consensus. Most users accepted the proposal; a minority did not. Since then, there have been two Ethereum blockchains: ETH and ETC. The latter being the original one that was not corrected. ETH users suddenly saw their tokens duplicated because they now exist in the old and new blockchains.

The curious thing is that the programmer never committed a crime; he just executed an available code, even if it was wrong. The blockchain, per se, continued to be as safe as ever; the fault came from the contract's programming.

Subsequently, two more bifurcations occurred, but without the same impact as the first one.

Currently, the Enterprise Ethereum Alliance (EEA), created in 2017, promotes the adoption and use of Ethereum in organizations and enhances its ecosystem to promote the development of new business opportunities.

The alliance comprises 159 members such as Accenture, Intel, Microsoft, ING Bank, Banco Santander, New York Mellon, CoinCircle, LG CNS, PricewaterhouseCoopers, Quanttstamp, and VMware, among others.

Remember the main points of this chapter:

Ethereum is a project created by Vitálik Buterin after verifying that Bitcoin has some limitations.

By means of a superior programming layer, it managed to extend the new token's functionality.

In 2016, the first ETH-based DAO was launched: a fully automated and decentralized management company where decisions are made based on a smart contract.
Due to a failure in the DAO programming, a subtraction of 15 million dollars was made. The solution adopted led to ETH's first hardfork. Since then, ETH and ETC coexist.

The Enterprise Ethereum Alliance (EEA), created in 2017, promotes the adoption and use of Ethereum in organizations and strengthens its ecosystem to drive the development of new business opportunities.

Chapter 7: Understanding Ethereum

"The technical side of Ethereum's efficacy is 100% an engineering exercise."

Vitálik Buterin, developer and Ethereum co-founder

Ethereum is nothing more than an open software platform on a blockchain. Being open-source implies that any developer can use, modify and distribute the code at will, with the richness that this creates both in the community of developers, in the improvement they create, and in the programming of new distributed applications called DApps. These are developed in languages such as Solidity, Servent, Mutant, Python, or Javascript and execute their code on the blockchain.

Like the Bitcoin network, the Ethereum initially used the Proof of Work as a consensus protocol. However, since December 1, 2020, when version 2.0 "Serenity" was released, it began to use the Proof of Stake (PoS) in the new Beacon Chain that manages the registration of validators for the PoS. When the Ethereum 2.0 network is fully deployed, it will be more scalable, allowing a higher number of transactions and energy-efficient. It will not be until mid-2021 that the implementation of PoS will be a reality. In the meantime, the blockchain using PoW will remain in place.

Ethereum also has its own "currency," the Ether (ETH), but it has a very different purpose than bitcoin. The purpose of the ETH is to be the engine that moves a decentralized mega-computer. This supercomputer is responsible for executing smart contracts.

There is a big difference in the circulation of bitcoins and ethers, since while the first limits its production to 21 million bitcoins, Ethereum has no limit in terms of the number of tokens. In any case, there is already talk of the need to set a maximum number. In April 2020, Vitálik Buterin set a figure of 120 million as reasonable and necessary.

As mentioned above, bitcoin's main difference is the existence of a top layer called the Ethereum Virtual Machine (EVM) capable of running complex algorithms, called smart contracts, on all nodes in the network. The fact that it runs in all the nodes implies a processing limitation. That limitation was 15 transactions per second in 2016 and will become 100,000 thanks to Serenity's arrival.

The Ethereum network is what in computer theory is called a "*Full Turing*." Any current computer is also one.

If in the bitcoin network blocks were created from a series of transactions, in the ETH network, some entities called accounts, which have a unique address and can store an ETH balance, are traced in the blockchain. There are two types:

Externally Owned Accounts (EOAs)

These are private key accounts that are controlled externally. They can't execute code, but they can trigger transactions. The private key is used to sign the transaction, allowing ETH to be consumed and contract code to be executed. Once signed, the transaction is sent to the network, thus propagating through all the nodes of the Ethereum.

Contract Accounts

These accounts have an associated programming code executed after the arrival of a transaction or a message from another account (contract or external). A message is similar to a transaction but produced by a contract account. They are a type of internal transaction.

Once a contract account is activated, it runs its code in the EVM on all the network nodes simultaneously. Basically, you have a routine that can have any complexity, running in every node. To avoid, therefore, the misuse of it, each operation within the network implies a cost called gas that must be paid with Ethers. That also avoids problems such as infinite loops due to wrong programming.

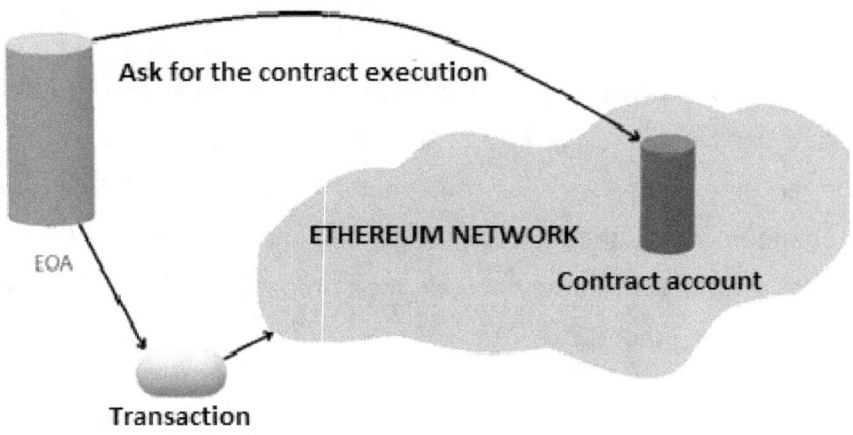

Figure 7.1 Transactions inside the Ethereum network

A certain amount of gas is paid for each step in the contract, so the more complex it is, the higher the price. Each contract will have an associated maximum cost in the form of gas, called the gas limit. Thus, when an external account opens a transaction, it must send an amount of gas to cover the costs (including those of validation and creation of the package by the miners) and, if after the completion of the transaction there is a surplus, it is returned to the issuer.

Each transaction is composed of:

- Issuer's signature.
- Receiver.
- Message (optional).
- Gas needed to transmit to the receiver.

- Gas price: price the issuer is willing to pay for each step. It is usually a little higher than the estimated cost, ensuring that the user accepts the transaction.
- Gas limit: maximum number of steps that the transaction is allowed to take. If the gas consumed exceeds the gas limit, all changes made are reversed.

The miners who validate a block receive the gas consumed to execute all the transactions included plus 2 ETH. Nodes that are about to generate a block receive a reward called an "uncle block."

It should be noted that while a bitcoin block has a fixed size of 1 MB, the size of the Ethereum blocks is limited by a maximum gas of 1,500,000.

Remember that mining will be possible as long as the PoW consensus algorithm remains in place. In 2021, if there are no further delays, the exclusive use of PoS will be definitively established, and the miners will only receive a small commission.

In the future of the Ethereum, the validators, who must possess at least 32 ETHs to perform this function, will be the ones to reap the rewards.

The more ETHs are included in the stake, and the longer they have been participating, the greater the probability of being selected as a validator. These nodes (more than 16,000 validations will be needed) will confirm the block and add it to the blockchain. For all this, they will get a reward. Ethereum 2.0

dispenses with mining to build a robust and secure system for which its participants will receive passive income. The miners will only receive the rewards related to the gas consumed in the transactions. Therefore, it is foreseeable that there will be a migration of miners from ETH to other platforms.

The validators' rewards will range from 1% to 19% and proportional to the amount of participation and inversely proportional to the number of validators. With this new model, no HW will be necessary for the average user. He will simply need a wallet in which to deposit the ETHs and participate in a pool. Furthermore, to participate in them, they will not need to contribute 32 ETHs but will do so with any amount. Your rewards will be obtained according to what you contribute.

In the end, the old mining is converted into a decentralized financial service through which passive income is obtained. It is a tool already used by some exchanges for other cryptocurrencies or, as will be seen in chapter 12, what Uniswap does with various tokens. Some critics think that, in the long run, the Ethereum network will lose its decentralization because of this mechanism. Time will tell us who is right.

Another substantial change in 2021 will be the fragmentation of the blockchain into smaller blockchains so that transactions can be executed in parallel. This mechanism, known as Sharding, will allow reaching 100,000 transactions per second.

Remember the main points of this chapter:

Ethereum is an open software platform on a blockchain.

It implements an EVM that executes the smart contracts in all the nodes of the network.

In its beginnings, it used PoW as a consensus protocol, although since December 1st, 2020, it started a migration to PoS.

The currency of Ethereum is the ETH, which allows the operation of the network and the execution of smart contracts.

There is no limit on the number of ETHs put into circulation, although this may change in the future.

Chapter 8: Smart contracts and DAO

> "Ethereum exists because it enables developers to write smart contracts better than Bitcoin in the near-term."
>
> Nick Tomaino, @1confirmation founder

Chapter 6 introduced the DAO concept (Distributed Autonomous Organization) and the hardfork adopted to solve the $50 million hacking derived from a smart contract programming problem. Since these two concepts make up the revolution within the revolution that blockchains already represent, they deserve an entire chapter.

DAO (Decentralized Autonomous Organization)

A DAO is a company where its management is fully automated and decentralized, where decisions are made based on a smart contract.

Therefore, to establish a DAO, the first thing to do is form that set of rules (smart contracts) by which it will be self-managed.

Once the rules have been made public, it starts a funding phase in which a certain number of tokens are put up for sale as if they were shares. Therefore, there is no hierarchy, but the weight of each participant's vote will depend on the number of tokens they possess. Tokens can also be used to reward certain activities or behaviors that DAO requires from users. Also, because they are tradable, they can be bought and sold in an exchange. Any transaction is recorded in a blockchain with all that this implies in terms of security and immutability.

When the organization begins its operation, all management decisions are made by consensus. Please note that any wrong decision taken in the initial rules, or even a security problem, cannot be corrected until a majority agreement is reached to establish the change in those rules. The necessary majority will be defined in the initial rules for the creation of the DAO. Those rules are always public.

If you want to be a shareholder of a DAO, you only have to buy DAO tokens. Depending on your tokens' relative weight in the total, your vote will have more or less value in a decision.

The main problem faced by DAOs is that, due to their recent implementation, there is no legislation on them, so legal and regulatory uncertainty is very high.

Nor is the effect of democratization on decision making negligible, although paradoxical, since a group of uninformed token holders could take the lead in changing the organization's behavior. Clearly, this type of DAO is doomed to failure by simple natural selection. That is why you must be very careful in choosing where to invest.

The best example of DAO today is probably the DASH project, a cryptocurrency in a decentralized network that offers immediate payments and private transactions. Decisions are made by the masternode network, which is accessible to everyone.

The masternodes store all the blockchain and are responsible for instant and private transactions. They are backed by guarantees in Dash, and, in return, operators receive coins. Unlike the bitcoin network, where the miner receives the total reward for adding a block to the network, in Dash, the reward is shared among the miners and the masternodes with 45% each, with the remaining 10% going to a system of subsidies called "treasury" for proposals that are sent to the network and voted on by the masternodes.

On Dash, the network's governance power is absolute, to the point that, if the results of the development team are not satisfactory, the network can vote to replace it.

SMART CONTRACTS

Although smart contracts are closely linked to the Ethereum network, in reality, their conception is much older (speaking in computer terms, of course). The person responsible for its creation was Nick Szabo in his article "*Smart Contracts: Building Blocks for Digital Markets*," published in 1996.

Nick Szabo proposed in 1998 a decentralized financial system that used common elements to bitcoin as blocks marked with a timestamp and generated with PoW. All that in a blockchain: BitGold that as b-money was never released.

For Szabo, a visionary of that time, almost every clause in a contract could be integrated into hardware and software so that non-compliance would be costly, or almost prohibitive, for the hacker.

He used as an example what he called the "early ancestor of smart contracts," the vending machine. The machine offers a product in exchange for coins collected every day, so the potential cost of breaking the machine is higher than the booty obtained by the thief. The machine with a simple software based on state machine (a 15 years old child could code that) establishes the rules that determine the user's relationship.

With the arrival of cryptocurrencies such as Bitcoin, which as Satoshi Nakamoto recognized, uses many of the features of BitGold, Szabo found a platform where to implement his smart contracts, since they need to run on a public key network that facilitates the voting mechanisms, and require a decentralized and open database.

A smart contract consists of three parts:

- Object of the agreement.
- Signatories or participants of the contract.
- Conditions that must be met by the contract participants, which are written in a programming language.

The applicability of smart contracts is infinite, as much as our imagination allows. Although a smart contract can work independently, it can also interact with other contracts creating nests that increase the complexity and application possibilities.

They offer us a new concept of economy in which the need for an intermediary is eliminated, reducing the possibility of a conflict that has to be taken to court and providing a significant saving because the need for reliable third parties such as notaries, lawyers, registrars, intermediaries, etc., are no longer necessary. Also, continuous improvement is easily implemented with the different iterations in which the code is developed. Of course, traceability and security are guaranteed by the fact of running on a blockchain.

As mentioned in the previous chapter, the two main problems faced by smart contracts are the legal and regulatory vacuum due to their recent implementation and technological and economic disruption, the danger of security holes in contracts or poor programming, and the "hyper-democratization of management" that can cause people without any knowledge to influence the content of the contract.

Let's imagine now a rental contract managed through a smart contract.

The contract would be composed of:

- Signatories: Landlord and Tenant.
- Object: Housing owned by the landlord and to be rented by the tenant.
- Conditions: After the monthly payment and the tenant's initial deposit (validated by the network and stored in a smart contract), the apartment's lock will only be opened with a code known only by the tenant. He will pay the monthly payment before the 5th of each month. If there is a default, the tenant has two months to update their payments. If there is a debt after this period, the apartment's lock will be opened only with the landlord's code. The contract duration is two years and can be extended by either party. If the tenant wishes to terminate the contract, he must give two months' notice, after which the deposit will be returned to the tenant, and the lock's code will be the landlord's.

All payments will be reflected in the blockchain, and there is no option for fraud.

As you can see, the figure of the intermediary becomes unnecessary. It is an automatic and regulated process. The network itself carries out the custody of the deposit.

That is a simplified example of what can be modeled with a smart contract. As detailed above, the applications are unlimited. They are logistics and traceability, custody, health, and financial systems the easiest to apply to develop.

Remember the main points of this chapter:

A DAO is a company where its management is fully automated and decentralized, and decisions are made based on a smart contract.

Any transaction is recorded in a blockchain.

All decisions about the changes on a smart contract are made by consensus.

The rules are always public.

If you want to be a DAO shareholder, you only have to buy tokens of the corresponding DAO.

The network's governance power is absolute in a DAO.

Chapter 9: Tokenization

> "Everything will be tokenized and connected by a blockchain one day."
>
> Fred Ehrsam, Coinbase founder

All the examples explained so far, except for the rental agreement in the previous chapter, have focused on the exchange of cryptocurrencies or tokens within a blockchain without paying much attention to the differences between them when, precisely, the most significant potential of blockchains lies in non-financial areas, which will see their businesses altered by the irruption of blockchain technology.

So, what is the difference between a cryptocurrency and a token? The answer is straightforward. The token concept is much more generic and can be applied to areas very different from the strictly monetary. Calling cryptocurrency to any token is a common mistake that should be avoided.

Chris Burniske, in his fabulous book "*Cryptoassets*," distinguishes between three well-differentiated types of cryptoassets, and I really don't think a better definition can be made:

- *Cryptocurrency*. It is a universal unit of exchange, value deposit, and unit of account (it measures the market value). Of course, the most prominent example is Bitcoin, but so are others like Litecoin or Dash.
- *Cryptocommodity*: as in the analog world, it represents the raw materials, which in the digital world are not wheat or oil, but the capacity and speed of transmission, hashrate, storage, or computing capacity, among others. This category's maximum exponent is the Ether, the fuel in the form of gas of the world's largest computer engine.
- *Cryptotokens*: represent services and digitized assets. An artwork or even a house could fall into this category. In this category falls those tokens exchanged by the DApps thanks to smart contracts, GEO's case, which is wholly dedicated to the following chapter.

The tokens that are financial securities deserve a special mention. In such a case, the product, like any other bond, share, or future, will be regulated by the corresponding competent authority (SEC in the USA and CNMV in Spain). Investors should only acquire this type of token with sufficient knowledge to access them, and therefore this characteristic should be checked in smart contracts. This type of token can only be issued by entities regulated by the authorities mentioned above.

Cryptotokens are, by nature, much more generic. They can accommodate any analog asset that comes to mind. But, what is this tokenization process, and how is it done? This chapter will answer those questions.

Tokenization is the process by which assets (or liabilities) are converted into tokens that can be recorded (even fractionally), stored, and exchanged in a blockchain. A smart contract performs this process. You, as a reader, could be thinking at this moment that the contract has to be smart because how can you know if the property belongs to who it says it is? Especially in assets such as real estate that may also have charges. Where do smart contracts get that information? The answer is straightforward, from another type of software called oracle.

Oracles are the blockchain's connections to the real world. They are programs that contain some libraries that allow them to connect to some centralized elements that keep certain information.

Let's see an example with a rental agreement simplifying the process:

Imagine that you own an apartment on the beach valued at 300,000 euros, and you decide to tokenize it to get an immediate return.

You decide to create 300,000 tokens of a 1 euro that give its owner a proportional share of the apartment's returns while it is rented or sold, if the token holders decide. You can put all of them up for sale or keep the majority share.

That raises questions for potential token buyers: Is the token owned by who it claims to be? Is it free of encumbrances?

At this point, the oracle comes into play, who will have the necessary libraries to connect to the Land Registry and check that the conditions announced by the seller are met. Once verified, the smart contract will be in charge of selling and transmitting the tokens through an ICO, as well as the corresponding monthly payments. These payments can be made with a cryptocurrency instead of tokens, if preferred. Each one of the investors will be identified by the smart contract, making use of the oracle they need for this purpose, generally the KYC platform (know your client), and is reflected in each transaction they make.

The tokens can be sold and transmitted in the secondary market. Once the property's renting or selling is over, the tokens will cease to exist and will have been exchanged for cryptocoin or fiat currency. Please note that token holders do not own the property but have rights to the benefits it generates.

You can see that there are certain similarities with the "splitting" into packages that banks make with their loans and mortgages.

There are platforms specialized in the tokenization of real estate assets. One example is Blocksquare, which creates and issues tokens linked to commercial real estate and distributes the rental income to hundreds of investors worldwide. With a P2P transfer system and without any intermediary, transactions are made automatically and quickly. It is worth mentioning that the company is established in Slovenia, where the legal obstacles are lower.

Today this concept is also applied to the tokenization of credit cards (Paycomet), in web browsers such as Brave, apps such as GeoCash that reward with tokens the transfer of anonymized data; to games such as CryptoKitties, dedicated to the world of the collection of kittens that can be bought and sold, or Upland, a parallel universe where you can buy and sell with tokens real estate in locations in our real world, and which can be exchanged for dollars in the future. In terms of services, the Spanish training platform Tutellus is worth mentioning.

It would also be possible to create tokens on the intellectual property to finance its edition and publication.

The benefits of tokenization are undeniable since they inherit all the blockchains and the smart contracts that run on them. On the one hand, security, traceability, immutability, and protection against fraud and counterfeiting are taken to the extreme. On the other hand, the costs associated with asset transfers are reduced as much as possible thanks to intermediaries' absence.

Thanks to the smart contracts, the speed of proceedings will be very high. They will be carried out almost instantaneously because all the bureaucratic formalities currently required for a sale and purchase will be eliminated, and everything will be reflected in the blockchain. Besides, the arrival of new investors is allowed when a property is divided into different tokens. It will even be possible to own 5% of a Picasso artwork's rights.

Of course, it will be fundamental when diversifying a portfolio. Thus, risk exposure will be controlled by including uncorrelated tokens with the rest of the portfolio's assets.

Although tokenization of analog assets is an unstoppable process, there are still obstacles to its implementation in the short term, especially in countries with high bureaucratic hurdles. The legal and regulatory uncertainty is what today slows down the definitive implementation of this economic model. In countries such as Spain, where a property's transfer must be registered in the Land Registry, a property's tokenization could be useless for practical purposes. To accelerate the implementation of this and other changes related to Fintech, several regulatory sandboxes (or regulated test environments where companies can test their products for a limited time) have been set up in different countries, such as the one established by the FCA in the UK. In Spain, on November 15, 2020, Law 7/2020 for the digital transformation of the financial system came into force, which included the implementation of a regulatory sandbox for fintech companies.

Remember the main points of this chapter:

There are three types of cryptoassets:
- *Cryptocurrency as Bitcoin*
- *Cryptocommodity as ETH*
- *Cryptotokens: represent digitized services and assets as GEO*

Cryptotokens are exchanged by the DApps thanks to the smart contracts.

They can represent any analog asset.

Tokenization is the process by which assets (or liabilities) are converted into tokens that can be registered

The oracles are the blockchain's connections to the real world to obtain specific information that is not available in the system.

Chapter 10: GeoDB

"The time has come to democratize the Big Data monopoly."

GeoDB

I already commented in the prologue of this book that GeoDB is to blame for my immersion in the world of blockchains. I reached them through a funding campaign published on the Crowdcube platform in 2019.

As I explained in my previous book, "*The Sustainable Portfolio*," I think it is very convenient to dedicate a small part of a portfolio to invest in startups. These are high-risk investments from which a high return is expected, and the fact that a company is financed through platforms such as Crowdcube or Seedrs gives certain guarantees about the project. The possibility of the company failing after four years is much lower in startups that manage to pass their filters.

GeoDB's proposal caught my attention. After so many years of giving my data to big corporations like Amazon, Google, or Facebook, GeoDB started offering a reward in exchange for what I was already giving for free. If users have been the most forgotten in the world of Big Data, GeoDB makes them part of it, and they also benefit from it. A new concept is introduced, the Big-Crypto, which is nothing more than the interconnection of the Big Data with the blockchains and the cryptocurrencies in an open ecosystem. It is a paradigm shift by which the end-user is considered an essential part of the industry and in which I saw high probabilities of success. At the end of 2020, it was consolidated as one of the leading European companies in the Blockchain environment.

GeoDB is the first ecosystem of P2P user data exchange (partially decentralized) on blockchain, using ERC20 tokens. Thanks to its smart contracts, the network rewards users for the anonymized data they deposit in it so that buyers can acquire sets of them. Both rewards and payments are made through the GEO token, which can be exchanged for fiat money on exchanges such as Bitforex or LongBit.

The total number of tokens amounts to 1,000,000,000, of which 100,000,000 remain as reserve, and for the equipment, 200,000,000 are for sale, and the rest (700,000,000) will be distributed as rewards for the smart contracts for 21 years.

It was operating in a test network during 2019 and 2020, rewarding users with test tokens to fine-tune the developments. In early 2020, the migration to the Mainnet started, and the test tokens began to be exchanged for real GEO tokens. Since the number of tokens generated was very high, it was decided to encourage the conversion in a phased manner.

During the test phase, the received support was spectacular, getting achievements that other companies in the same sector couldn't do it. Among others, the following stand out:

- Three successful financing rounds at Crowdcube and Seedrs where the amounts initially planned were exceeded, leading to overfunding.
- A community with more than 125,000 members with a high level of Twitter participation (28,000) and Telegram (82,000).
- In October 2020, the number of data blocks reached 1,250,000.
- More than 250,000 downloads of its application, GeoCash, in more than 150 countries by the end of 2020.
- More than 160,000 active wallets with more than 600,000 transactions.
- Incorporating its GeoFarming platform, a liquidity incentive mechanism generated more than 600,000 GEOs as a reward with a stake of more than $300,000.
- Positive references in media articles such as Investing.com and Tech Times.
- Collaboration agreements with leading companies such as Grupo Next, Wola, or Wave.

ODIN Introduction

The most exciting development was announced in December 2020: The new ODIN protocol will mean evolving from a semi-centralized platform to a decentralized blockchain open protocol. It will become a DAO formed from their community that will govern the network after its launch. Implementation on the Mainnet is planned for the end of 2021. It will be possible to interconnect with other oracles and marketplaces, extend the types of data supported, and introduce decentralized data storage and computation within the system.

Before continuing, I have to thank GeoDB for let me use its whitepaper as a source for the rest of this chapter.

The primary purpose of ODIN is to create a data oracle network and to build a decentralized peer-to-peer data sharing and trading ecosystem. Its primary objective is the assurance of the decentralization, giving the oracle network the following three characteristics:

Permissionless

Everybody can become a data provider within the system's limits. To do this, a transaction must be started to create a new data source, in which it is determined how this source can be accessed. This way, it enables, for example, model creation that allows thousands of data sources and allows the end-user to choose the sources he wants to use. Firstly, it is needed to remove the threshold that establishes who can be a data source.

Validation

The information transfer process is decentralized. No single party transfers data from all sources to the system, but many validators access the data sources with the same requests and create reports on the information obtained. These reports are aggregated and become the input for all other data operations. Thus, the tolerance to attacks is multiplied exponentially, eliminating a vulnerable point that could endanger the system's integrity.

Open

As it is an open system, anyone can suggest an improvement in the data processing algorithms received. The end-user can choose the most suitable one for him, according to the price, reputation of data sources, etc.

The protocol's three characteristics were achieved thanks to an architecture composed of 3 different roles, a governance token called ODIN, the oracle scripts, dPoS as a consensus protocol, and treasury.

Roles

The new role system allows any user to become a contributor and receive rewards. The roles are as follows:

- *Validator.* It is one of the main roles of the system, as it participates in the consensus protocol. Its main functions are the formation, proposal, verification, and confirmation of the system blocks. Besides, they receive data from external sources and generate reports.
- *Delegate.* They are participants of the networks who want to become a validator, who will be those having more votes (stake) from users.
- *Auditor.* According to the protocol's rules, they maintain a complete copy of the blockchain and check all blocks and transactions. They don't take part in the consensus protocol.

Oracle scripts

Oracle scripts are smart contracts that can be used by all participants in the system to establish how data from external sources is received and processed. Any participant can develop them.

Native token

ODIN uses its native token (ODIN) for network governance and operation to reward validators for creating blocks and responding to data requests.

ODIN holders can use it to pay for data received from the network, become validators, participate in the network's governance, and delegate it to a validator to earn the proportional share of the fees and rewards obtained by the latter. The annual inflation rate for validators staking is set to around 12% APR. After ODIN launch, GEO to ODIN swap will be available for GEO holders with 24 months vesting period. Notice that the ODIN:GEO ratio is 1:50. During this period staking to validator nodes only is available. After this period, tokens are unlocked for 12 months evenly daily.

The total supply of ODIN is limited at 100 million tokens with the following distribution:

- Data consumers pool — 10%.
- Staking and validator's rewards — 30%.
- Company & founding team — 10%.
- ODIN treasury — 50%.

Governance

ODIN holders may participate in the network governance with a weighted vote on their stake. The main decisions are related to the governance protocol's rates and limits and system parameters and data oracles changes.

Any token holder can request protocol upgrade proposals by sending a particular type of transaction in which the changes will be defined.

Treasury

ODIN's Treasury is a key financial tool, especially in the first stages of the project, when the data oracles will be still semi-decentralized. At that time, the treasury will collect payments from data consumers in ODIN tokens that will not be used for the governance.

Therefore, the treasury's primary purpose will be to sell ODIN tokens to the market participants and collect payments in other cryptoassets like ETH, BTC, etc. 80% of these collected payments will be used to buy GEO via auction; every time soon 800 USD threshold is achieved, acquired GEO tokens will be allocated to the recycling pool for future use as a means of payment to data providers. The other 20% will be invested in DeFi following the decisions taken by consensus.

With the ODIN protocol publication, GeoDB positioned itself as one of the most promising companies within the Blockchain scope, which will presumably be reflected in the GEO token's value.

Remember the main points of this chapter:

> GeoDB rewards users who share their anonymized data through its GeoCash app with GEO tokens.
>
> It implements a new paradigm in the Big Data that considers the user a benefited part of the business.
>
> GEO is an ERC20 token. The smart contracts will determine when and how much users are rewarded based on the shared data.
>
> 1,000,000,000 tokens will be distributed, of which 700,000,000 are dedicated to rewarding the user.
>
> It uses liquidity incentive mechanisms that reduce the GEO token's financial risk and offers the user very high returns.
>
> The new ODIN protocol will mean evolving from a semi-centralized business model platform to a truly decentralized blockchain open protocol becoming a DAO.
>
> The three main ODIN characteristics are:
> - Permissionless.
> - Open Protocol.
> - Validator role.
>
> The main roles will be:
> - Validator.
> - Auditor.
> - Delegate.

> ODIN uses its native token (ODIN) for network governance and operation.
>
> It will be deployed on the Mainnet in late 2021.

Chapter 11: Altcoins

"Cryptocurrency is absolutely here to stay. If you can't see that at this point, it's time to learn more about it."

Joel McLeod, Premivm.com founder

This chapter focuses on the alternative cryptocurrencies to Bitcoin. Since ETH and GEO have been explained in depth in previous pages, they are not included in this chapter.

There are currently hundreds of altcoins on the market, and the following lines are dedicated to the main ones. The vast majority of altcoins' goal is to improve one or more features that Bitcoin doesn't cover in a satisfactory way (volatility, speed, etc.) or are tokens that, as explained above, serve a purpose defined by a smart contract.

Currently, according to CoinMarketCap, there are more than 2,200 tokens and more than 1,000 cryptocurrencies.

Aeternity

Aeternity is a project launched in 2017 by Yanislav Malahov as a very ambitious computing and digital asset platform based on Blockchain. The project aims to improve the efficiency of the current blockchains. It is focused on games, exchanges, and micropayments, among others. The AE token, Aeternity's own, is used to reward miners and as a gas for smart contracts and transactions.

Aave

Aave is a decentralized lending platform that allows users to access credits and lend cryptoassets without intermediaries. It works on Ethereum. Initially, the LEN token was used, but a migration to AAVE is underway.

Augur

It is a project created on Ethereum to generate reports with predictions on different markets from specific indicators. Users participate in the creation of these predictions. The production version was launched in 2018. Its REP token is used to reward users who generate accurate forecasts.

Basic Attention Token

BAT is one of the most exciting projects in the current market, and of which I am a convinced user. Launched in 2017, it introduces a paradigm shift in advertising consumption in web browsers and runs on an Ethereum. Brave browser allows users to decide whether to view ads or not and rewards them for their viewing with BAT tokens. Advertisers, publishers, and users can exchange these tokens. It is used as a collateral for DAI.

Binance Coin

It is the token (BNB) of the Ethereum-based Binance exchange founded by Changpeng Zhao. It finances its projects and grants certain benefits to its holders in discounts on their commissions. Besides, it has a beneficial function; the possibility of converting the small remains of other unused cryptocurrencies after a purchase or sale operation and exchanging them for BNB. This way, they can be used in another operation or exchanged for another crypto.

Bitcoin Cash

In 2017, a Bitcoin hardfork occurred because many developers thought the miners' rewards were too high and saw a clear need to improve efficiency. The fundamental difference is that its blocks are 8 MB. The name of this cryptocurrency was Bitcoin Cash (BCH)

In December 2018, a hardfork was produced that resulted in the creation of Bitcoin SV.

BCH suffered another fork a few days before the writing of this chapter. On November 15, 2020, Bitcoin Cash ABC (BCH ABC) and BCH Node (BCHN) began to coexist. A group of Bitcoin Cash developers led by Amaury Sechet proposed an update of the Bitcoin Cash Network, which has included a new rule, requiring that 8% of the cash extracted from the Bitcoin mines be redistributed to BCH ABC as a means of funding the development of the protocol.

Bitcoin Diamond

BCD is another of the bifurcations that Bitcoin has suffered throughout its short history. As in the previous case, the reasons were the same: high mining commissions and slow transactions. This hardfork took place in November 2017, and everyone who owned bitcoins at that time got BTC, the ticker of this new cryptocurrency, in a 10:1 ratio.

Bitcoin Gold

BTG emerged as a response to the criticism of centralization that bitcoin mining was beginning to suffer. As described in previous chapters, mining farms tend to be concentrated in countries where electricity costs are meager. For this reason, the protocol used as a PoW is changed. The bifurcation was made at the end of 2017.

Bitcoin SV

It's the result of a hardfork suffered by Bitcoin Cash. According to their website, "*Bitcoin SV is the original bitcoin. It restores the original Bitcoin protocol and will keep it stable, scaling it to a mass level. Bitcoin SV will maintain the vision proposed by Satoshi Nakamoto in his 2008 technical report "Bitcoin: A User-to-Authority Electronic Cash System."* Its ticker is BSV.

BitShares

BitShares is a decentralized exchange created by J. Chitty, who designed a financial derivative called BitARS, whose underlying is the Argentine peso (ARS). The objective is to use it to create and finance projects related to the crypto world in Argentina and, if necessary, as a common currency.

BlackCoin

The BlackCoin project was one of the first to change the use of PoW for PoS to solve scalability problems in the blockchain. BLK holders that is their ticker receive 1% per year for holding their coins.

ByteCoin

It was born in 2012 to offer absolute privacy. Transactions are made between totally anonymous entities so that payments made with them are not traceable. Its ticker is BCN.

Cardano

It is a platform similar to ETH since it uses smart contracts, which has its main claim scalability and speed. It uses PoS instead of PoW. The token used in Cardano is the ADA.

Celsius

The Celsius project's objective is to offer financial services without commissions, reduced interest rates, and speedy transactions. It was approved by the SEC and by the British Companies House to operate as a financial entity. It was created in 2017 by Alex Mashinsky and Daniel Leon. A year later, it started to operate. It uses CEL token as a claim to obtain substantial discounts on its products.

ChainLink

ChainLink is a decentralized oracle network that allows smart contracts from any blockchain, public or private, to access real-world data. Its token, LINK, has experienced very significant growth in recent times. Its purpose is to encourage participation in the network honestly since oracles can only receive payments with this token. It has a positive projection due to measures that have not been implemented yet, but very interesting, like the derivative contracts, which require a very high deposit and increase the interest for the oracles to accumulate LINK. The company was founded in 2017 by Steve Ellis and Sergey Nazarov.

Cosmos

The Cosmos project, created by Jae Kwon and Ethan Buchman in 2014, is supported by the InterChain Foundation. It aims to create a blockchain of blockchains as the network of networks that is the Internet. Each separate blockchain is called a zone. The first blockchain, called the Blockchain hub, keeps a status record of each zone and vice versa. The Cosmos Hub uses PoS as a consensus algorithm and the ATOM token to maintain activity. In this way, the nodes compete to validate a block according to ATOM's amount, thus encouraging demand.

Crypto.com Coin

Crypto.com is a blockchain-based exchange and payment platform for cryptocurrencies that can be accessed through its website and a mobile application. It also offers credit cards. It is possible to deposit cryptocurrencies and obtain a return of up to 6%. Payments are made weekly.

According to its whitepaper, founded in 2016, its mission is to accelerate the global transition to cryptocurrencies and tokens. CRO is the native token of this blockchain, which uses PoS. Besides, having CRO provides advantages in the exchange and payment platform.

Dai

Maker is a DAO on Ethereum, founded in 2014 by Rune Christensen and launched to the market in 2017, that conforms a financial platform whose primary purpose is the protection against the cryptocurrencies volatility, for which it uses the DAI, that replicates to the American dollar maintaining a stable exchange against it. It is a stablecoin crypto-collateralized thanks to the smart contracts of the network. Also, the MKR token is used to pay fees to the participating nodes in the network.

DasCoin

It's a blockchain similar to Bitcoin that uses a PoW consensus protocol variant to improve commercial transfers. It incorporates KYC to verify clients and vendors or senders and receivers. It also aims to fight against the volatility present in almost all cryptosystems. DasCoin (DASC) mining is much more efficient than Bitcoin mining with the consequent reduction in electricity consumption. It was introduced to the market in 2018.

Dash

Dash coin is a currency created in 2014 and officially launched in 2015. Dash is the acronym for Digital Cash. That's what it aims to be: a direct competitor of Bitcoin with specific improvements such as faster transactions and the ability to send or receive money completely anonymously through the use of a network of master nodes. It can be found on all major exchanges under the DASH ticker.

Decred

Decred is a blockchain launched at the end of 2015 whose objective is to create a digital currency superior to the rest and of automatic governance, whose rules can be changed by consensus by the whole community. It uses a mix of PoW and PoS protocols, using the percentage of currency (DCR) to weigh the proposals' vote in its platform.

DogeCoin

The DogeCoin project was launched in 2013 by Billy Markus and Jackson Palmer. Born from a Litecoin hardfork, it takes the Bitcoin philosophy and aims to expand it to a much larger audience, using friendlier environments. The cost of the transactions is minimal, and they are done very quickly. It's oriented to small payments since it allows you to send a minimum of 0.00000001 DOGE. For this same reason, it is the cryptocurrency chosen by many faucets to reward the user for completing tasks.

Electroneum

The Electroneum project aims to fill a gap between the payment gateways through smartphones. It is being oriented to a public that lacks access to bank offices. ETN is a currency born in 2017 that could only be mined in the Electroneum blockchain with a mobile phone. Some media claim that the mining was not real but a simulation by which ETNs were sent to the "mining" terminals to keep the project active. There is currently a platform for freelancers (AnyTask) that can be used to perform tasks and obtain coins in exchange. It is considered a very safe and low energy consumption blockchain, which uses the Proof of Responsibility consensus protocol.

EOS

EOSIO is a project launched in 2017 as an alternative to Ethereum. It is a platform for developing applications on a blockchain with smart contracts in which very complex programs can be developed. EOS, its token, is the equivalent to the Ether in Ethereum.

FirmaChain

This blockchain aims to replace all written contracts (notarial, registration, purchase and sale, legal) with electronic documents stored in the blockchain. To do this, you need the documents to be digitized in an encrypted manner and uploaded to the platform through its web or mobile application. All this is done through the use of a DApp called E-CONTRACT. Its token, the FCT, is required to pay for the DApp services and be exchanged for FDR, the token used by FirmaChain's decentralized storage system. FDR or Firma Data Reward is the reward paid to blockchain miners.

Golem

Golem is a blockchain created by Julian Zawistowski in 2016 that acts as a supercomputer. Suppose someone needs to execute a costly task, so much so that it is not easily executable on an ordinary computer. In that case, it is possible to pay a fee in GNT (native token) to access its services.

Huobi Token

Huobi is a significant decentralized exchange in Asia. In 2018, it decided to create a new token (HT) to market on its platform and serve as an incentive with discounts on its products. Besides, online purchases can be made through the FomoHunt e-commerce Platform

Icon

According to its website, ICON is a decentralized network created in 2017 that allows users to connect to any blockchain. Thanks to this network, communities that were previously disconnected can now connect and share services. It is one of the main gateways between blockchains. This blockchain uses PoS as a consensus protocol, and its token is the ICX.

Libra

It is possibly the project best known by the general public. It is a platform proposed by Facebook, resident on a blockchain that will allow different cryptoassets. Its objective is to create a global currency and an infrastructure that allows millions of people to share it. The Libra currency will be linked with 1:1 correspondence to a fiat currency, in principle the US dollar. Real assets will back it. Here lies the controversy: it will be the Libra Association responsible for managing the platform and determining its future. Thus you say goodbye to decentralization.

Litecoin

It is the "lite" version of the Bitcoin. It was created in 2011 by Charlie Lee. It has many similarities with its "big brother," such as using the PoW protocol. Transactions with LTC are faster, and the cost is really reduced. When the last litecoin is issued, there will be a total of 81 million coins in circulation

Lisk

It was launched in 2016. According to its official site, Lisk is a Blockchain application created to bring blockchain technology to the real world through an SDK written in JavaScript, the most common programming language worldwide. Lisk (LSK) is the token offered in the ICO with which the project was financed. Also, it is used to pay transaction costs. LSK holders can vote on decisions made on the platform.

Monero

It is a Bytecoin fork that appeared in 2014. It is one of the most used cryptocurrencies for your privacy since all its operations are anonymous, including all the participants' IPs in a transaction. To this end, all its wallets have a public and a private address. The blockchain uses PoW as a consensus protocol and rewards its miners with their currency (XMR ticker).

NEM

NEM is an advanced blockchain that allows you to create applications on it and offers a feature that others do not have: the ability to create a decentralized network from any system. Programmers can work on a private blockchain (or a public one) that uses the Proof of Importance as a consensus algorithm due to its need to make scalability effective. Its native currency is the XEM.

Neo

Erik Zhang and Da Hongfei's project was created in 2014 as Antshares and renamed in 2017 as Neo. It is a blockchain-oriented to digitalizing assets through smart contracts that provide digital identification through X.509. It allows the creation of applications on it using the NEP-5 standard. The virtual machine on which its smart contracts run is called NeoVM. The token used in the network is the NEO, which cannot be mined because it uses PoS. It has become in its own right a rival to Ethereum to be reckoned with.

OKB

It is a currency created by OK Exchange. It is a token that runs on Ethereum. 50% of the service fees obtained by the exchange are divided proportionally among OKB holders.

OMG Network

The OMG project emerged in 2017 to respond to the scalability problems of Ethereum, improving it by adding a new layer to its architecture. In 2018 the network was migrated to a blockchain of its own with Plasma architecture. The network's token is called OMG.

Polkadot

Polkadot's goal is to be a gateway between other blockchains, whether public or private. It uses PoS as a consensus algorithm so that nodes that store DOT (their token) can perform validation tasks and be rewarded for it. It was founded in 2016 by Gavin Wood.

Ripple

The company Ripple was founded in 2015, although the work on the protocols began years ago. It is responsible for creating a blockchain that allows creating one of the most efficient payment systems worldwide. Due to this, many banks and financial institutions make use of it. Adopting the XRP currency reduces the cost of operations to users. Its purpose is mainly commercial.

Stellar

It is an open-source system for P2P payments based on Blockchain. It allows payments with low commissions between different currencies using an intermediate currency called Stellar Lumens (XLM).

In addition to the payment gateway, it offers a set of tools such as Kelp, which allows you to create markets through a trading bot.

Tether

It is an Ethereum-based blockchain whose token (USDT) replicates the behavior of the USD. It cannot be undermined; it was created solely to serve as a stable value cryptocurrency concerning an underlying dollar. The main advantage it has is the lack of correlation with the rest of the cryptocurrencies, so that if USDT is kept in the portfolio during a fall in the crypto market, the USDT will continue to have the same value.

Tezos

It is a company founded in 2014 that launched its blockchain of the same name in 2017. The blockchain forms an application development platform on smart contracts that uses an alternative consensus algorithm called Liquid Participation Testing, which requires a small threshold of tokens for a node to be validated. The token name is XTZ.

TRON

It is a company with one of the most ambitious objectives of the last five years: the Internet's decentralization. In the beginning, Ethereum was used as a blockchain, but now it uses its blockchain that uses the Delegated Proof of Stake (dPoS) consensus algorithm. The token used is the TRX, which is used to pay the expenses incurred in the network. Besides, it is the currency used in business operations within the network.

Uniswap

Uniswap is a decentralized exchange created in 2018 by Haydem Adams, allowing token exchanges and runs on Ethereum. It creates liquidity pools that are rewarded with an interest rate, allowing investors to make token exchanges. The return is determined by the percentage of participation in the pool applied to the fees that have been incurred for each trade. Its token is UNI and is used to entitle its holders to the management of Uniswap.

UNUS SED LEO

It is the cryptocurrency created by the Bitfinex exchange in 2019. It is used to offer discounts for transactions made with LEO.

USD Coin

This cryptocoin deserves a special mention. It is possibly a good entry platform for those who are suspicious of the crypto world. It is a currency that maintains the same value as the US dollar. The difference with Tether is that a real dollar backs each USDC. The

Circle consortium, based in Boston, is in charge of tokenizing the dollars and maintaining parity.

VeChain

VeChain is a blockchain platform focused on traceability in supply chains, registering a product from its creation to the moment of its sale, going through all the transformations it undergoes. It uses Proof of Authority as a consensus algorithm so that the block validating nodes are not anonymous but must be approved. All operations are paid with the VET token, including the miners' shares.

Wanchain

It is a platform created by Dustin Byington and Jack Lu in 2017. Although it used the Ethereum network, it currently runs on its own blockchain that uses PoS. The platform's objective is to intermediate between other blockchains that allow exchanging different currencies without any problem. Its token, the WAN, is the equivalent of the Ether in the Ethereum. It is the engine of transactions and smart contracts. As in ETH, you can create decentralized applications on it and create tokens.

Waves

Waves is a blockchain that was born in 2016 at the hands of its founder Alexander Ivanov. It is a decentralized platform that allows users to create smart contracts without advanced programming knowledge and therefore create their own tokens. In this way, it facilitates the financing of new projects. The blockchain is based on LPoS (similar to PoS), which needs less energy and does not consume "gas" in Ethereum. WAVEs are accumulated to decide who adds a new block. Besides, the token is used to access the services of the platform.

Wrapped Bitcoin

It's part of the Wrapped Tokens project. It intended to create a token representing bitcoin in Ethereum. Therefore, a wBTC token is exchanged at a ratio of 1:1 by BTC or, instead, to generate a wBTC, you must store a bitcoin and vice versa. Thanks to this token, it is possible to access smart contracts of the Ethereum network using bitcoin. Its primary disadvantage is that its BTC custody system is centralized, so its security is significantly reduced.

Yearn.finance

It is a decentralized finance platform (DeFi) built on blockchain, which launched its native cryptocurrency (YFI) in July 2020 with unprecedented success, reaching over $32,000.

Its original idea was to serve only as a voting weight for YFI holders, but investors have been willing to buy it en masse, given the project's solidity.

Zcash

It's a Bitcoin-based blockchain with the addition that it allows you to increase the privacy of transactions. It was created in 2015 by Zooko Wilcox. In addition to making the sender and receiver's privacy possible (optionally), the costs are meager. Its currency is the ZEC.

0x

The 0x project was founded in 2016 by Amir Bandeali and William Warren to create a platform to build distributed exchanges. They created the 0x protocol to create such exchanges through DApps based on the use of smart contracts on Ethereum.

The 0x token, whose ticker is ZRX, is used to compensate the transactions to the nodes that execute the contracts, called relayers. Besides, holders of this token can participate in the network management.

As you've seen, there are many altcoins, each with its peculiarities and improvements over Bitcoin and Ethereum. The ones presented here are easily available at any exchange. If you want to go deeper into it, you can visit CoinMarketCap and access the listings of the most important tokens and cryptosystems, as well as relevant information about them.

Remember the main points of this chapter:

Altcoins are the alternative currencies to BTC, such as ETH, LTC, or GEO.

The vast majority of altcoins' goal is to improve one or more features that Bitcoin doesn't cover (volatility, speed, etc.) or are tokens that serve a purpose defined by a smart contract.

Currently, according to CoinMarketCap, there are more than 2200 tokens and more than 1000 cryptocurrencies.

SECTION III: INVESTMENT

Chapter 12: Decentralized Finance

"Distributed ledger technologies such as cryptocurrencies and digital assets are shaking the system."

Christine Lagarde, economist and ECB president

At this moment, you can describe what a blockchain is and the mechanisms of Bitcoin and Ethereum. You also understand what tokenization is, and you know a good amount of cryptoassets. You can never learn too much, it's true, but my technical background makes me pragmatic. Acquiring new knowledge without getting paid for it is like going on a diet or doing sports without improving marks or the physical condition. For me, it is a wasted effort; that is why I prioritize the study of new concepts that give me some return. This same philosophy has led me to write the third section of this book. Once you have finished reading the following chapters, you will be able to open an account in one or several exchanges, stake crypto to a liquidity pool, and take advantage of many of the benefits offered by decentralized finance.

Already in my first book, I warned the reader to beware of some mistakes that can be costly:

- Invest the money you may need in the short term.
- Concentrate all your investment in a few assets or those that are correlated.
- Invest in a product or project you don't know about.

These mistakes made in the DeFi can cost you a significant headache. If possible, since the crypto world is a very volatile and high-risk world, you should only dedicate a small part of your investment portfolio, which will be bigger or smaller depending on your profile.

This section can be considered as the continuation of my first book, "*The Sustainable Portfolio.*" If you need to acquire and strengthen concepts about profitability and risk, diversification and portfolio construction, it would be convenient to read it before putting into practice the contents learned here.

Thanks to decentralization, eliminating the need for a reliable third party, smart contracts, and cryptography, a new form of investment has emerged that we could not imagine just a few years ago: The DeFi (Decentralized Finance). The name refers to the capacity of structures such as blockchains, or DLTs in general, to offer decentralized structures that support new financial services that do not include intermediaries, thus lowering costs and multiplying the range of products that can be accessed, as well as the number of people who can contract them. Also, at least for now, they are out of the reach of political decisions, which is good news, not only because of their influence but also because of the avoided bureaucracy.

Since DeFi uses smart contracts to operate, it is clear that the first steps were taken in the Ethereum network from 2016. Keep in mind that if you were to become an expert in this area, the person in the world with the most knowledge and experience would only have a 4-year advantage over you, which is fascinating. Not many times throughout history, these circumstances occur. They would be equivalent to those experienced by the people who understood and took advantage of the Internet's importance or those who decided to undertake in the Americas after the discovery. In the latter case, without the annoying inconveniences of a three-month journey across the Atlantic in a small wooden boat, the dangers of confronting the natives, being eaten by any animal in the jungle, or being infected with any deadly disease.

The importance of the DeFi is such that the real scope they could reach and the products they can offer is not yet known. Economists agree that DeFi is here to stay and will increasingly gain market share and force a change in the current way of investing, managing, and understanding finance worldwide.

As Christine Lagarde said, "*Distributed ledger technologies such as cryptosystems and digital assets are shaking the system.*"
Since the first DAO (The DAO) appearance, which despite the initial fiasco can be considered the first decentralized finance organization, the variety of DeFi platforms and products that can

be accessed is growing every day. This chapter will detail the most important ones.

It should be noted that the level of decentralization is not the same for all platforms available on the market. Thus, while Uniswap is a decentralized exchange, Binance is a centralized platform that allows access to tokens' purchase and sale from other centralized and decentralized platforms and blockchains.

Although Binance is a company that can be trusted, it is not exempt from risks derived from its centralization.

The main problems they present are the susceptibility to attacks and the need to trust the customer because, at any time, the institution could change the conditions without any impediment and, in the worst case, disappear with the money. Also, due to the high volume of traffic they support, they can become saturated for some time. For example, we can mention Bithumb, which has presented problems since it was hacked in 2019 and is currently under investigation by the South Korean police on suspicion of fraud.

For these reasons, faced with a centralized or decentralized system, we should opt for the latter.

PLATFORMS

0x

As noted in the previous chapter, 0x is a platform that emerged in 2016 to facilitate the creation of decentralized exchanges by using the 0x protocol, which is free and open-source, for programmers and companies to develop decentralized products for buying and selling cryptotokens.

Augur

Augur is a platform that allows report generation with predictions of different markets from certain indicators through a P2P protocol on Ethereum and an oracle designed for this purpose. In this way, the information passes from the real world to the blockchain world without a trusted third party. Users participate in the creation of these predictions. The production version was launched in 2018. Its REP token is used to reward users who create accurate predictions. Like the previous one, it is oriented to developers or companies that wish to deepen decentralized products' development.

From now on, only platforms that are accessible to the general public will be presented.

AAVE

The first of the platforms presented here will allow you to access loans and deposit cryptographic assets in exchange for a return. As commented in the previous chapter, initially, the LEN was used as its native token to vote for improvement proposals, but a migration to AAVE is underway. If you have AAVE, you could stake to facilitate the migration receiving 400 AAVE per day.

Users can deposit a certain amount of a cryptoasset (of those accepted in the platform), and from that moment on, you will receive passive income based on the demand for loans. Besides, if you need to apply for a loan, you can use your deposit as collateral to obtain better conditions.

The funds deposited are stored in a smart contract that carries a risk of protocol failure, although it has been audited.

They vary between 0.00001% and 0.09% regarding commissions, depending on whether it is for a deposit or a loan. When running over Ethereum, there will be some gas cost, which will depend on how the ETH network is when you make the transaction.

Figure 12.1 AAVE. Deposits

Figure 12.1 shows how the annual interest offered by deposits ranges from 0.07% for ETH to 104.84% for sUSD.

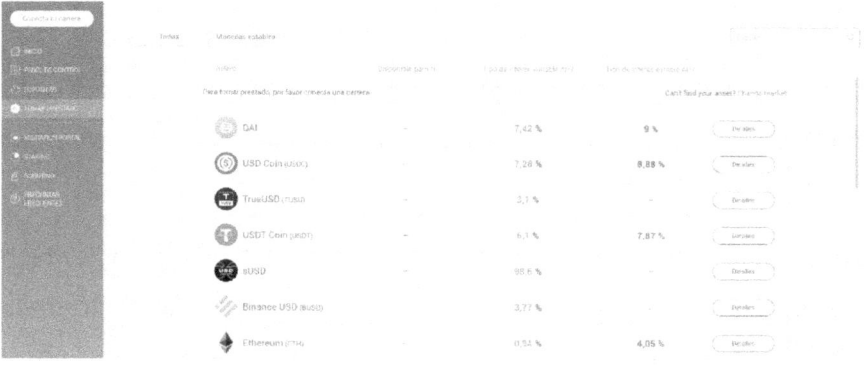

Figure 12.2 AAVE. Loans

As for the loans, variable interest is offered in almost all cases. Once again, a significant difference is observed between the 0.84% per year of the loan linked to ETH and the 98.6% linked to sUSD.

Torque

It is a similar platform to the previous one in which it is possible to access loans and deposits with the main difference that only fixed interest rates are offered on perpetual debt. That is, they have no end date. A loan is settled when the position falls below the maintenance margin. Borrowers are individuals who wish to use their digital assets to build leveraged positions.

The interest paid to lenders comes from the fees borrowers pay to access liquidity when trading on margin.

Compound

It is a lending platform that allows users to both deposit and request cryptocurrency. The operation is similar to the previous ones.

A depositor contributes a certain amount of cryptoassets for which he receives an established return when the product is contracted. The funds are allocated to a pool where users who wish to apply for a loan make their requests. All users who decide to make a request must offer a guarantee (generally with another cryptocurrency). In the case of Compound, the guarantee is greater than the money borrowed.

The interest generated by the borrowers goes to the depositor.

The operation would be as follows:

A user applies for a $1,000 ETH loan and puts up $1,100 in BAT as collateral, hoping that the ETH value will rise above the loan's interest. In this way, he obtains benefits. It is a form of leveraged investment.

Coinrule

It is a centralized platform that offers the user the possibility of automating their buying and selling operations (cryptoassets) based on their strategies. Its user interface is intuitive. It is possibly the best strategy automation platform currently on the market.

They have not launched any ICO. First, they have not needed the money because they have the support of large companies like RBS and, second, a currency of their own would not contribute anything to their platform.

You can open a free account with which you can automate two rules connected to a single exchange. With the pro account, for about $30 a month, you can automate seven rules on two different exchanges. It is not a DeFi platform per se, but it can be very helpful.

Young Platform

Young Platform is an ecosystem born in Italy in 2019, designed as an entry platform for investment in the crypto world.

Thanks to its app, Stepdrop, you can get Young (YNG) tokens simply by actions such as walking, passing tests related to the crypto and blockchain world, and getting the right predictions about the crypto money trend. It is fascinating the learning section. After reading specific articles and answering the final questionnaire, you will receive some tokens proportional to the correct answers. Although the rewards are small, it is an essential incentive for people to train before making their first investment.

The tokens obtained can be used in its exchange, Young Platform, which allows the purchase of crypto with fiat money and the exchange between cryptocurrencies. All this, in a very intuitive way. The most advanced users should use Young Platform Pro, which offers competitive features and rates. It is one of the best exchanges in terms of technical analysis indicators offered.

Besides this, if you live in Italy, you could go shopping and pay with YNG. It is not a decentralized platform either, but it can be an excellent gateway to the crypto world and DeFi products.

Voluto

Voluto is the DeFi alternative to savings accounts, with the substantial difference that the interest offered is up to 6%. Thanks to decentralization, there are no intermediaries or third parties. Funds can be withdrawn without any penalty at any time.

Contributed funds are invested in a cash pool on the Compound platform, a global and open virtual network of depositors and borrowers. Thus, the former contribute funds and obtain interest immediately, and the latter are the ones who, after obtaining their loan, generate interest for the former.

Borrowers must offer some asset as collateral to increase security for depositors. Interest rates are variable and depend on supply and demand.

As in all cases mentioned in this chapter, there is a risk associated with smart contracts development quality.

To use it, it is necessary to download the application from the app store of your mobile operating system.

Stake.fish

It is a decentralized platform that allows tokens' contribution in blockchains that use the PoS (Proof of Stake) consensus protocol. Stake.fish is a professional validator that allows users to stake to receive an annual return.

It is currently possible to stake in Ethereum, Polkadot, Tezos, Cosmos, and Cardano. Annual yields range from 0%-20% in Polkadot to 7%-20% in Cosmos.

yEarn.finance

If the yEarn.finance ecosystem finally met its expectations; it would be simply the greatest. Not surprisingly, its token, the YFI, has been priced at over $32,000.

It offers us a conglomerate of DeFi products and services within reach of a few clicks on the same intuitive website.

The products offered are divided into the following sections:

- *Earn*: Allows you to deposit stable coins and wBTC and invest them in yield farming; the same application is responsible for distributing them to those with higher profits. The interest received is fixed, and it is established when depositing the assets.
- *Zap*: Allows to exchange cryptocurrencies
- *Vaults*: It is similar to the Earn option, but it allows to invest stake tokens that have been obtained in a liquidity pool. In the next chapter, we will show an example

- *Experimental*: Space for experimental Vaults.
- *Stats*: Statistics on the performance of the Vaults.
- *Dashboards: This shows the graphics related to the user's portfolio.*

Lightning Network

It's a payment platform that uses Bitcoin transactions and smart contracts to create bidirectional payment channels between different blockchains. To make use of the network, it is necessary to have a Lightning Network wallet.

LN Markets

It is a tool that allows trading derivatives that can only be accessed through Lightning (a payment protocol that runs on Bitcoin). An expert trader can generate significant capital gains, but it presents such a high risk that it is not recommended for the general public. In my previous book, I warned that leveraged products are not recommended for a novice investor.

It can be said that the main advantage is for short selling on an asset, but I repeat that it is an option for investors with years of experience.

Etherisc

It is a decentralized platform created by a German company that allows insurance products through smart contracts on Ethereum.

It currently offers various products such as flight delay insurance, hurricane protection, electronic wallet theft, crop protection, and collateral protection in loans with cryptocurrency.

Uniswap

Uniswap is one of the DeFi projects with the greatest projection of the moment. It is financed by the Ethereum Foundation, which is a significant support, not so much for the economic figures, but for the strength it brings to the project. It is a decentralized exchange that allows exchanges (swaps) between ERC20 tokens using a liquidity pool instead of the book of purchase/sale orders of any classic exchange (or any stock exchange).

The idea is surprisingly simple. A liquidity pool is created for each of the token pairs that can be exchanged, for example, ETH-GEO. The liquidity providers are the users depositing ETH-GEO token pairs and obtain a return for it through the commissions of 0.3% or 0.6% on the swap's cost (depending on whether at least one of the tokens exchanged is ETH or not). Those are the users who want to make a token exchange. Also, the trader will have to pay for the cost of the gas. All this results in a decentralized, robust, very secure system and much lower commissions than any centralized exchange.

Liquidity providers can make very high profits. In the case of ETH-GEO, returns of over 1,000% per year have been achieved, although today, at the end of 2020, the return is around 200%, which is not insignificant.

Profitability depends on the combination of two factors, liquidity and volume, according to the following rules:

- *High liquidity and volume*: An average return would be obtained since many commissions will be earned thanks to the high volume, but the swap's price will be low because of the high liquidity.
- *Low liquidity and volume*: A medium return would be obtained because few commissions would be earned due to the low volume and a high swap price.
- *Low liquidity and high volume*: High yield because many commissions would be obtained due to the high volume with a high swap price due to the lack of liquidity.
- *High liquidity and low volume*: This is the worst-case scenario. The yield would be low because of the few commissions obtained due to the low volume and a low price due to the high liquidity.

It is an open-source protocol that uses smart contracts on Ethereum, which has facilitated the production of hardforks with which Sushiswap arose, explained in the next section.

Sushiswap

It is a decentralized exchange that emerged in mid-2020 with remarkable success. So much so that it managed to block more than a billion dollars in just five days and made the price of gas at Ethereum soar. I bear witness to it because I was one of the injured parties in my operations in August of that year.

Sushiswap is a branch of Uniswap that offers more generous rewards to its community and with a native token used for its holders to vote on decisions to be made on the network. The main difference with Uniswap is, therefore, in governance. Uniswap is not centralized means that only a few people remain as managers of the protocol, thus obtaining great benefits. For its part, Sushiswap has decentralized its network's governance, which means that power and money remain in the blockchain's hands. In this way, users who maintain Sushi tokens earn passive income. The costs are similar in both exchanges.

To obtain tokens is very simple; only Uniswap tokens must be deposited in its smart contracts. In this way, through yield farming, sushi tokens are obtained. Due to this mechanism, Uniswap's aggregate liquidity has grown significantly since the advent of Sushiswap.

As cons, the number of currency pairs that can be exchanged at Sushiswap is significantly lower, and it is an unaudited project with all the risks that this entails.

Binance

Binance is one of the leading exchanges in the world. Although it is centralized and not part of the DeFi world, it is worth noting that it allows the purchase and sale of cryptoassets from other centralized and non-centralized systems. Founded in China in 2017, it is one of the most intuitive and easy to use. It sells derivative products, allows the deposit of currencies in a liquidity pool and access to loans. It allows to exchange fiat money for cryptocurrencies by credit card, debit card, and bank transfer, and its commissions are reasonable. It can be used as a digital wallet where to store the different cryptocurrencies it allows to exchange.

In the previous chapter, we described Binance's native token's particularities and the advantages for its holders.

It is possible to access Binance Academy, where tutorials, courses, and other learning material about cryptocoins and blockchain are included from its web.

CoinBase

It is one of the leading platforms for exchanging cryptocurrencies, together with Binance, with more than 35 million verified users. It belongs to CoinBase Inc, a company founded in 2012 in San Francisco by Fred Ehrsam and Brian Armstrong. Like Binance, it is a centralized exchange that provides the user with a wallet address that can be used as a virtual wallet. Through its Coinbase Commerce application, it allows companies to receive cryptocurrency payments.

It currently allows the purchase and sale of Bitcoin, Bitcoin Cash, Ethereum, Ethereum Classic, ETC, Litecoin, XRP, 0x, USD Coin Stellar Lumens.

Bitforex

BitForex is a company based in Hong Kong but registered in the Seychelles. It offers a secure crypto trading platform. In addition to buying and selling cryptotokens and cryptocurrencies, it allows trading derivatives. Its internal token is the BF token, which allows the user to benefit from lower commissions. Along with Binance and Uniswap, it is one of my favorite exchanges.

Binance P2P

It is the peer to peer exchange version of Binance. You can request to buy or sell at a certain price and wait for someone to come to the operation. It is necessary to register on the platform, which means goodbye to anonymity, but reduces the possibility of fraud to a minimum. The coins' price can vary by 20% up and down compared to the cryptocoins' real price.

It presents a mechanism of appeal to which to resort in the event of a dispute between the two parties. In such a case, Binance P2P would act as an arbitrator.

Opyn

It is a (non-custodial) derivatives and options-based DeFi risk management platform founded by Zubin Singh Koticha. The primary use of these derivatives is to cover a purchase or sale operation of cryptoasset with the option to buy or sell at a previously defined price so that if a purchase operation is successful, the option to sell the same asset at a lower price would not be effective, losing only the price of the option. If the sale transaction is a loss, the sale option will become effective at a lower price than the initial one, and the benefits would be maintained.

It also offers protection against smart contract failures.

LocalBitcoins

It is a P2P exchange platform founded in 2012 and based in Finland. It does not have any kind of limitation on the purchase/sale price as Binance P2P does. Both sellers and buyers can make their bids while waiting for it to be fully addressed. That is because a buyer can only purchase part of the amount offered by the seller. The cryptocurrencies offered by the seller remain in the custody of the platform until the sale is effective.

USEFUL TOOLS

Coinmarketcap

Coinmarketcap is the best website to access information as relevant as the market capitalization, which is calculated by multiplying the circulating supply by the current price.

The most important indicators that can be consulted are: market capitalization, circulating supply, total supply, and maximum supply.

Since investment strategies are not the book's subject, their explanation will be left for the next book series.

Bitcoinwisdom

It is an exchange that can be used merely as a technical analysis platform, being one of the most complete on the market.

Blockfolio

It is a fundamental tool for portfolio tracking. It helps to make buying and selling decisions and can be connected to the leading exchanges.

Coingecko

It is one of the best tools to perform a cryptoasset fundamental analysis. In addition to market capitalization, it includes indicators such as the progress of a project and its community's growth. It even provides data on the code status through GitHub tracking.

INVESTMENT PROPOSALS

Throughout this chapter, the possible investments that can be made in the crypto world have been outlined, but in this section, they will be explained in more detail.

ICO

It is the acronym for Initial Coin Offering, through which cryptocoins, generally tokens, are sold to finance a project linked to the token. Investors turn to this type of mechanism, hoping that demand will cause the asset's price to rise in the future.

It is considered a very high-risk investment since it could be the case, as has happened in the past, the developers abandon the project, and the tokens take on zero value. Simply put, it would be the equivalent of buying shares in a startup seed. For this reason, it is essential to study the project well before embarking on one of these adventures.

There are also intermediate alternatives. As a small investor in GeoDB and the purchase of shares, I received an incentive in the form of tokens from the company.

HODL

The original term is hold, but it became famous because of a misspelling by a drunk BitcoinTalk user. Later it was considered to be the acronym *Hold On For Dear Life*. It takes all sorts... It´s purchasing cryptoassets waiting for an increase in their future value without investing in an additional product.

Yield farming

Users with cryptotokens can obtain returns passively through this mechanism in which a user deposits assets in a pool that is available to other users who will request loans. Depositors obtain their benefits from the rates or fees generated and the interest generated. All users who decide to make a request must offer a guarantee (generally in another token), which is usually more significant than the requested amount.

On the other side, a user applies for a $1,000 ETH loan and provides $1,100 as collateral in another token, hoping that the ETH value will rise above the loan's interest. In this way, he obtains benefits. It is a form of leveraged investment.

One of the most suitable platforms for this purpose is Compound.

Liquidity mining

It is a variant of yield farming where the depositor is rewarded for a feature of the protocol. He is awarded governance tokens and seeks to increase liquidity in the system. In this way, if the governance token value rises, more yield will be obtained, which will have a knock-on effect for other users who will provide greater liquidity, again improving the protocol's benefits and increasing the governance price token. That is the so-called virtuous circle of liquidity mining and the reason why Sushiswap enjoyed a meteoric rise in its early days.

Staking

With the arrival of the PoS protocol as a consensus algorithm, the door is open to passive income generation in a very different way to mining. Thus, the blockchain validating nodes with higher amounts of tokens will have higher probabilities of validating a block.

The rewards can be calculated in many ways, and it depends on the particular blockchain on which the staking is done. It can be a fixed percentage over the amount of participation, or over the time of validation of the node concerning the total, or simply a fixed amount of coins.

Some exchanges have a staking pool where the profits are distributed among the participants.

There are several types of staking offered by exchanges, but the most common are the following two:

- *Locked*: The user locks his cryptoassets for a fixed period and obtains returns in return. The longer the blocking time, the greater the benefit obtained.
- *Flexible*: in exchange for obtaining a lower return on investment, there is the possibility of obtaining passive income without establishing a fixed blocking period. Instead, the funds can be withdrawn when desired.

Derivative products

Derivative products are financial instruments whose value depends on how their asset prices evolve. They allow, among other things, to be short against an asset and are susceptible to being leveraged since a small investment is needed compared to the exposure to which one is subject. They are high-risk products that should only be used by experts. If you finally decide to trade with this type of product, one of the most recommended platforms is Opyn.

Stablecoins

The stablecoins arose from the need to mitigate the volatility that most cryptocurrencies suffer, exceeding 10% intraday, making trading strategies seriously difficult. They are cryptocurrencies that replicate a fiat currency (the American dollar in almost all cases) and maintain collateral for this task. The vast majority of stablecoins have as collateral the American currency itself, but others, such as DAI, use cryptoassets (ETH and BAT) to keep the exchange rate fixed.

The easiest way to invest with stablecoins is to buy another asset such as BTC or ETH, hoping that its price will rise, thus obtaining benefits and considering that the operation will result in losses if the price drops. If, besides, it is done with leverage, losses and gains can be multiplied.

It is also possible to deposit stablecoin in platforms such as Compound and get a return for it.

The last alternative would be to borrow and get a return for it (as detailed on previous pages).

You can apply for a loan of 1,000 DAI, for which you need to collateralize between 120% and 150%, depending on the platform. Thus, you would deposit as an ETH guarantee equivalent to a minimum of $1,200 to participate. If the ETH increases in value by around 20%, you will have $1,400, and, also, you will have used the borrowed DAIs in another operation that would have brought you a profit, such as a deposit. After returning the borrowed DAIs and paying the commissions, the profit is above 20%.

It does take advantage of the rest of the cryptosystems' volatility compared to the stability of the Tether, DAI, or other stablecoins.

Insurances

The benefits of the decentralized insurance platform Etherix, which allows the creation of insurance products through smart contracts that run on Ethereum, have already been mentioned above.

Currently, it offers a wide variety of products such as flight delay insurance, hurricane protection, electronic wallet theft, crop protection, and collateral protection in loans with cryptocurrency.

Another firm to consider is Nexus Mutual, which also runs on Ethereum and offers coverage against smart contract failures and computer attacks.

EXCHANGES

It is essential to stop and talk briefly about exchanges since their operation can lead to confusion, especially regarding their functioning the final price of cryptoassets.

The first surprise that a user who decides to buy a cryptocurrency such as bitcoin receives is that its price is not the same in all the exchanges, but depends on the supply and demand in each of them is no official price. The price that can be read in the news responds to an average of the leading world exchanges' purchase price. Although these could alter the price, the law of supply and demand and free-market makes the price similar in all of them, since investors move from one to another depending on the profitability they can obtain.

But what is an exchange? It is a platform where you can exchange cryptocurrencies (or cryptotokens) for others, and in centralized ones, also these for fiat money. Therefore, if you are new to this world, you will have no choice but to go to a centralized exchange to buy cryptotokens with euros, pounds, dollars, or any other currency by credit card or bank account, among other methods. Most exchanges also allow access to other products such as deposits, loans, yield farming, or derivatives.

As mentioned throughout this chapter, there are two types of exchange, centralized and decentralized. Both have advantages and disadvantages. It is recommended that newcomers to this type of investment use the former until they have a thorough understanding of the latter. Another option for these users is to contract an investment fund whose underlying is cryptocurrency. If it is a passive fund, the commissions will be low, which may be worth it. In any case, the following chapter will show you how to make your first investments directly on a centralized exchange and another that is not.

Centralized exchanges

The main characteristic of a centralized exchange is that an intermediary is needed to execute the desired transaction, which has repercussions on the lack of privacy of the transactions, the risk of theft or hacking simply because sensitive information is centralized in a "single point.," and the fees charged are higher. There is also the danger of embezzlement of deposited money. However, the positive side is that their interfaces are friendlier; liquidity is generally higher, and they offer more products. As a rule, this type of exchange offers to exchange for fiat money.

The vast majority of major exchanges are centralized. They arrived earlier and took more market share. Also, their ease of use and product portfolio make them more accessible to the general public.

The operation of these exchanges is what governs the stock markets. According to this book, there is a book in which offers and demands are introduced, and transactions are carried out.

Attention should be paid to the commissions charged by this type of exchange since they are usually high and vary significantly from one to another.

Decentralized exchanges

Decentralized exchanges use protocols on blockchain and intermediate a third party to carry out the transaction unnecessary. Any company does not retain contributed funds or customer information, and they perform the exchange of cryptocurrencies through the use of liquidity pools. As mentioned in the previous section, liquidity on this platform is lower than on centralized ones. They have fewer products and, above all, they are much less friendly for the end-user. As a counterbalance to these disadvantages, it presents much lower commissions, privacy and security are much higher if the risk associated with protocol failures is obviated. That is especially true for those who are not audited.

By way of conclusion, it can be said that the DeFi have come to be more and more deeply and extensively implemented. The fact of eliminating intermediaries in the transactions, maintaining more advanced security standards than those of the current financial mechanisms makes the trend irremediably optimistic. That is also helped by the ease and accessibility for a public that until now has not been able to access certain products and that, thanks to the DeFi, will be able to do so. Besides, the returns offered are far higher than those obtainable with a classic financial product.

The associated risks have been commented on throughout this chapter and the previous ones: high volatility, lack of legislation on the subject, unreliability of unaudited protocols, governance problems, precisely because of the democratization of the management of DeFi, and, last but not least, the number of scams that exist for example with some ICOs that have been launched. For all these reasons, we must keep in mind four fundamental rules for every investor:

- Invest only the money that is not needed in the short and medium-term.
- Since they are a risky investment, only a small percentage of the portfolio should be dedicated.
- Only participate in investments of known products, so it is necessary to study the project or product you want to invest in.
- Prioritize diversification against high short-term gains.

Remember the main point of this chapter:

> **Mistakes that can be very expensive:**
> - Invest the money you may need in the short term.
> - Concentrate all your investment in a few assets or those that are correlated.
> - Contribute money to a product or project you don't know about.
>
> The crypto world is a very volatile and high-risk world to which you should only dedicate a small part of your investment portfolio, which will be more or less depending on your profile.
>
> The importance of DeFi is such that the real scope they could reach and the products they can offer is still unknown
>
> The level of decentralization is not the same in all the platforms available in the market
>
> Faced with the choice of a centralized or decentralized system, we should opt for the latter.
>
> The main products offered by DeFi platforms are
> ICO, exchange, trading and margin trading, deposits, loans, yield farming, staking, derivative products, and insurance

Chapter 13: Real cases

> "You don't learn to walk by following rules. You learn by doing and by falling over."
>
> Richard Branson, Virgin founder

Everything described so far in this last section makes no sense if it is not put into practice. Therefore, this chapter will show, step by step, how to carry out the primary operations that can be done with cryptocurrencies and DeFi.

In the previous chapter, different exchanges (centralized and decentralized) and P2P platforms were presented. It is highly recommended that the reader choose one of the platforms mentioned above or, if not, study any other alternative to avoid becoming a victim of any fraud.

If you decide to use a centralized exchange platform such as CoinBase or Binance, you can use your virtual wallet and leave it in the hands of a third party. This book advocates keeping the custody of the wallet and the private key to maintain independence. That entails a high responsibility because, in the case of the private key's loss, all the funds stored in the wallet would also be lost.

The following is a description of the main types of wallets you can use.

Physical wallet

They are usually made of paper or metal and contain a public address, where cryptocurrencies are stored, and a private key allows access to their content. They can be generated using services such as Bitcoinpaperwallet or by buying them directly from sellers such as Amazon (which is not advisable). If you choose the paper version, you must take the necessary precautions to avoid deterioration or loss. Their only advantage is that they are immune to computer attacks but can be easily lost.

Hardware wallet

It is the safest option when it comes to storing cryptocurrencies. They are devices connected to a computer through a USB port and are designed to prevent any type of computer attack. They can be acquired for a more than fair price (from around 50 euros). A recommendable option could be the Nano X Ledger.

Mobile phone wallet

Since mobile devices are easily hackable, special care must be taken if using this type of wallet. You should avoid coexisting with other applications developed by unrecognized companies.

Within this category, TrustWallet stands out, allowing the storage of a great variety of tokens and cryptocurrencies. It is compatible with most decentralized exchanges.

Plugins

These are extensions for web browsers such as Chrome. MetaMask stands out, a plugin developed by Aaron Davis and Dan Fiblay in 2016, allowing Ethereum DApps with Google's browser, Firefox or Brave, among others. It serves as a wallet for ETH and tokens of the Ethereum network.

In summary, for large volumes of currencies, the best solution would be to choose a hardware wallet. Simultaneously, it would be best for day-to-day operations to use a mobile wallet such as TrustWallet or MetaMask in case it works with tokens from the Ethereum network.

Please note that the operations described below may incur losses. Therefore, please note that:

- You should only invest a small percentage of the equity portion of your portfolio.
- Depending on your risk profile, the equity portion should be between 10-15% and 80% of the total.
- Do not invest money that you may need in the short or medium term. The volatility of cryptoassets is very high.
- Invest only in those products you know. Spend the necessary time studying what you are planning to invest in.

FIAT-CRYPTO/CRYPTO-FIAT EXCHANGING

The first and easiest operation that a cryptoasset investor can make is the acquisition in exchange for fiat currency. There are three possibilities to do this:

Purchase at an ATM

It is a straightforward option that can be carried out by credit or debit card. In the search engine coinatmradar, you can find the nearest ATM to your place of residence. Pay attention to the commissions you may be charged because they vary substantially from one to another.

Not all cryptocurrencies or tokens can be acquired through this procedure. Generally, you will find the following:

- Bitcoin (BTC)
- Bitcoin Cash (BCH)
- Ether (ETH)
- Dash (DASH)
- Litecoin (LTC)
- Zcash (ZEC)
- Monero (XMR)
- Dogecoin (DOGE)
- Tether (USDT)
- Ripple (XRP)

After inserting your card in the ATM, you must indicate the amount of currency to be withdrawn, as well as the address of the wallet where you want to deposit it.

The inverse operation is also possible, selling your cryptocurrencies and making the deposit in your credit/debit card. Remember that sales commissions are higher than purchase commissions.

P2P exchange

It is the cheapest and most profitable option, because you can make purchases with very significant discounts, and the most insecure and exposed to fraud. If you decide to use this option, we recommend that you use the Binance P2P platform. The transactions are not anonymous, and it offers an arbitration service, so the possibility of fraud is much lower.

Purchasing on an exchange

Since it would be your first cryptocoin purchase, you have no choice but to make it in a centralized exchange. Decentralized ones, as a rule, do not allow the exchange of fiat currency.

In this case, Binance will be used as an example because of its friendly web and the ease of payment by transfer within the EU.

The first thing you have to do is register yourself as a user by entering your email address and a password. After receiving a confirmation email, you will be able to use the platform both on the web and in your app.

Once inside, you must access the "Buy Crypto" drop-down menu and select the "Bank Transfer" option (figure 13.1). As you can see, this type of purchase does not have any type of charge or commission. The only drawback is that it will take one or two days for your funds to appear in your Binance account. After indicating the amount you wish to transfer, you will obtain the bank account number to which you must remit the amount and the concept to be included in the transaction to link the payment to your user.

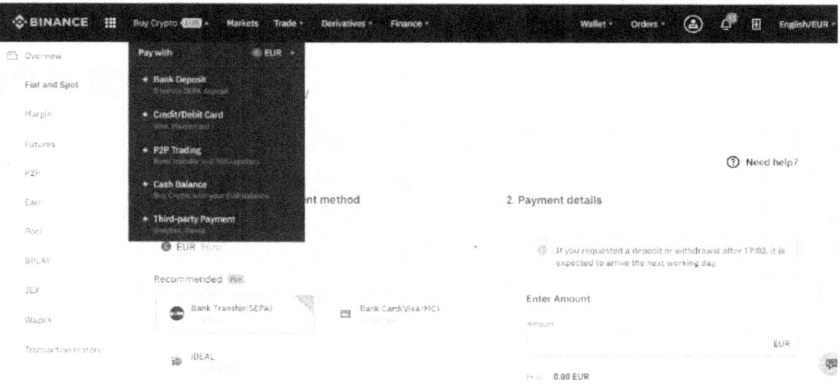

Figure 13.1 Binance. Buy crypto

If you want to start trading immediately, you will have to choose to purchase by bank card or use the iDEAL platform (if you have an account). In such cases, you will be able to directly buy cryptocurrency (ETH, in this case) (figure 13.2).

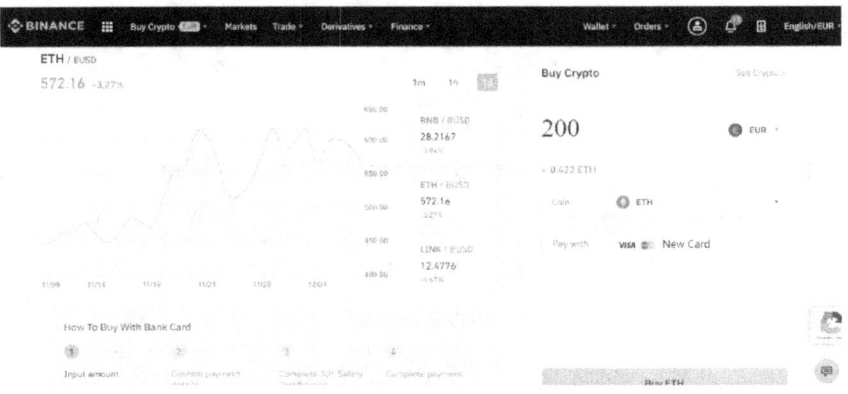

Figure 13.2 Binance. Crypto purchase with credit card

In any case, the option recommended by both me and the platform is the bank transfer.

Once you have the funds in your Binance wallet, you will be able to purchase crypto. In the example, an ETH purchase will be made. Figure 13.3 illustrates the simplified trading screen offered by the exchange. Note that the charts are displayed at the day level. This detail is critical, and you should do the same if you want to invest in the long term.

The upper right-hand list shows the pairs that can be traded. Since the objective is to buy ETH, the ETH/EUR pair will be selected. Just below the chart are the "Buy" and "Sell" sections. You must go to the left section and select SPOT and Limit Buy. If you make a market buy, you will get the cryptocurrency at the best possible price offered at that time, but it is usually not the best option. Instead, you should look at the chart and check the patterns. It is advisable to obtain notions of technical analysis to make purchases at the best possible time. In this case, you should wait until the value is close to the 25-day average, so the purchase is ordered for a price close to €458. If you look at the chart, three lines appear below the candles that indicate the asset's daily behavior. The 25-day average is the central line.

In a situation like the one shown in the chart, Slightly more advanced investors would include a stop-loss 5% below the purchase price.

Figure 13.3 Binance. Trading platform

Since the ETH price will most likely fall to that price, the order will be filled throughout the day. In case it does not, you can adjust the order or revoke it and create a new one.

Once the transaction is executed, the ETHs (at the corresponding fraction) will be sent to your wallet.

Investors, a little more advanced, would not buy in the current conditions unless they are trading, that is, do not make long or medium-term investments. The best method for purchasing this type of asset is crossing 5 and 70-day moving averages (or 9 and 21 for medium-term investment). In a simplified way, it can be said that when the average of 5 crosses over the average of 70 in an ascending way, it would be a purchasing signal, and if it did it in a descending way, it would be a selling signal. A stop loss of 5% below the price at which the cryptocurrency is acquired would have to be applied.

To select the moving averages in the chart, you must click on the icon with the shape of a wheel indicated in figure 13.4.

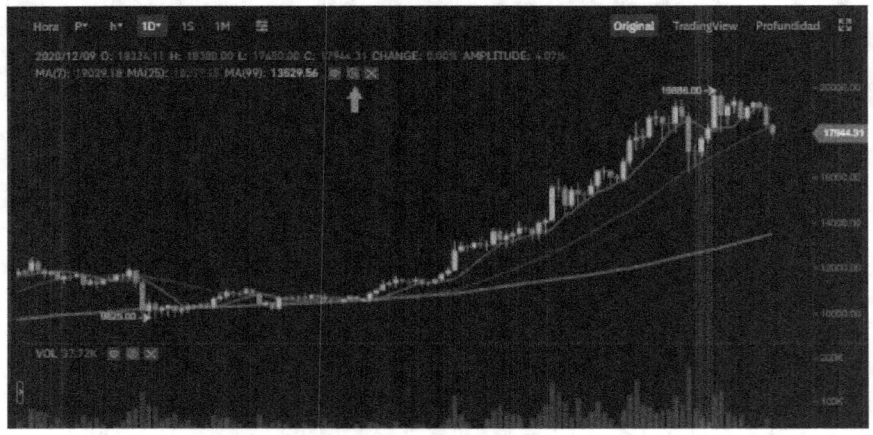

Figure 13.4 Binance. Trading platform configuration

A window will appear over the chart where you can enter which moving averages you want to display. Enter 5 and 70 in the corresponding boxes (figure 13.5).

You can include up to three different moving averages for a single chart. If you want to include all three, we recommend 5, 70, and 100, respectively.

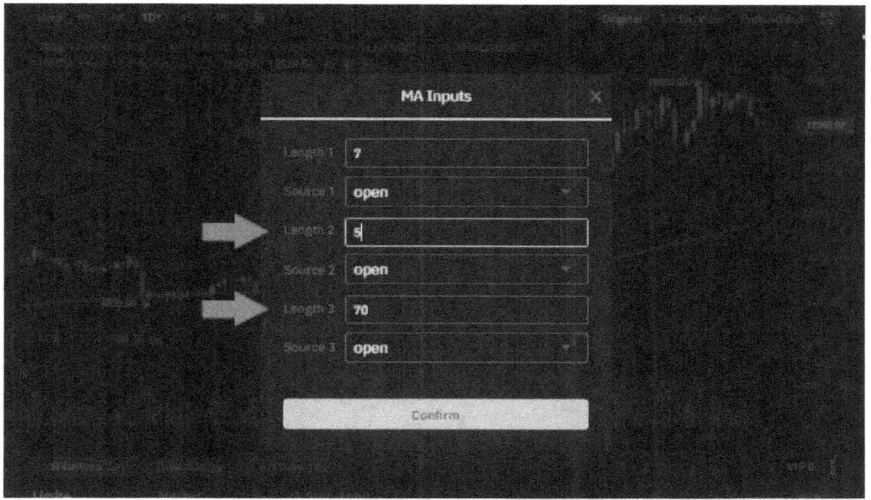

Figure 13.5 Binance. MA configuration

After confirming the changes, the averages of 5 and 70 days are drawn on the screen. In figure 13.6, you can see how the current moment is not the most suitable to buy because the last crossing of moving averages of 5 and 70 in a bullish way is very far on the y-axis.

It is easy to see how the chart has given three trading signals since September 2020. The first, at the beginning of September, and the third, in mid-October, are buying. The second signal is for sale. You can see that the crossing of averages has been a reliable indicator for trading in all cases. Note that, although it is in most cases, it isn't always this way. For this reason, you should always make your purchases with a stop loss that you cannot afford to lose.

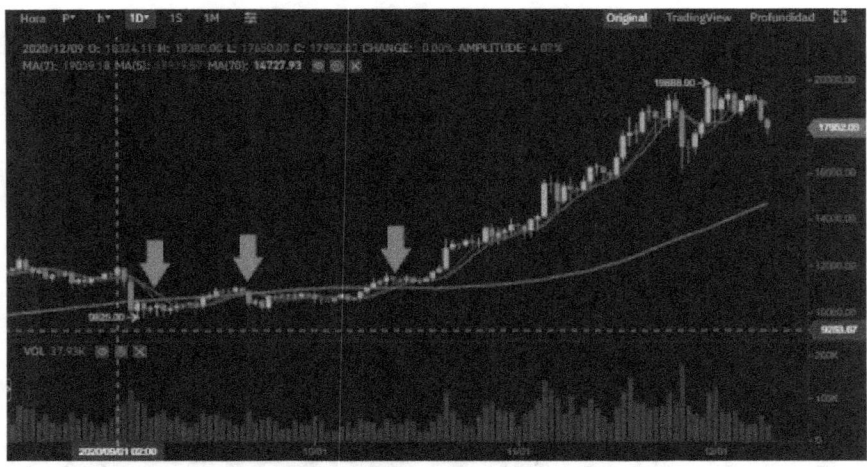

Figure 13.6 Binance. MA crossing

The sales process is similar to the one outlined here for the purchase. You simply need to invest the chosen pair (EUR/ETH in this case), execute the transaction and send the euros back to your bank account.

CRYPTO-CRYPTO EXCHANGING

The process of exchanging crypto for crypto is the same as in the previous case, except that a crypto-crypto exchange can also be done in a decentralized exchange. The fees will be much lower, and the security is greater because we do not depend on an entity that holds the assets.

The following example describes how to acquire GEOS by exchanging them for some of the ETHs purchased in the previous section, using Uniswap.

The first thing to do is use a TrustWallet or MetaMask wallet, which are the best for working with ETH ERC20 tokens. In this example, the second will be used. You can install it on your cell phone, but it is recommended that you use the existing plugin for Google Chrome. You can find the link to download and install it at www.metamask.io (figure 13.7).

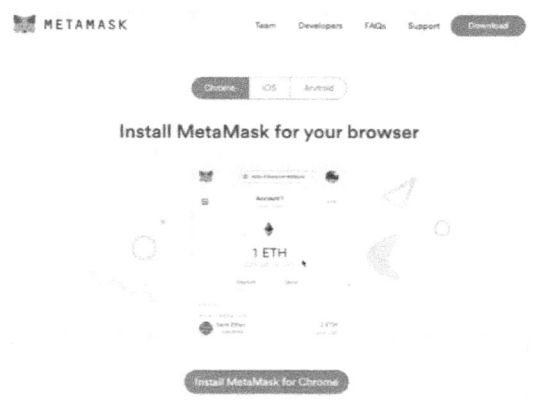

Figure 13.7 MetaMask. Installation

Select the browser where you want to install it and click "Add to Chrome." See figure 13.8.

Figure 13.8 MetaMask. Add extension

Once the plugin is installed, you will need to enter a password to access the system (figure 13.9). That password must be unique. That is, do not reuse the same one from your e-mail or any other. For your own security, you must comply with some basic rules such as the following:

- Do not use names or surnames (yours or those of family members).
- Do not include dates.
- Do not use words from the dictionary.
- Must contain alphanumeric and special characters.
- It must be at least eight characters long.

If you find it difficult to remember your password, you can always install on your computer a tool such as KeePass, which makes this task easier.

Below, MetaMask offers you a list of twelve words sequenced in a specific order that will help you retrieve your wallet address if you forget your password. Copy it and keep it in a safe place.

Figure 13.9 MetaMask. Password

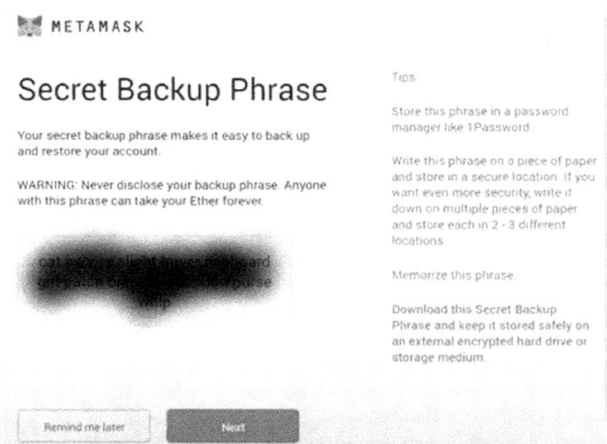

Figure 13.10 MetaMask. Secret backup phrase

In the next window, you will be asked to confirm that you know all twelve words by including them in a text box. Remember that the order is as important as using the valid words.

After clicking on accept, you will be able to access your new wallet for the first time. As you can see in figure 13.11, it is an almost diaphanous window composed of two main panels.

First, you must make sure that the wallet is connected to the Ethereum's main network, for which you will only have to click on the drop-down menu in the upper right corner.

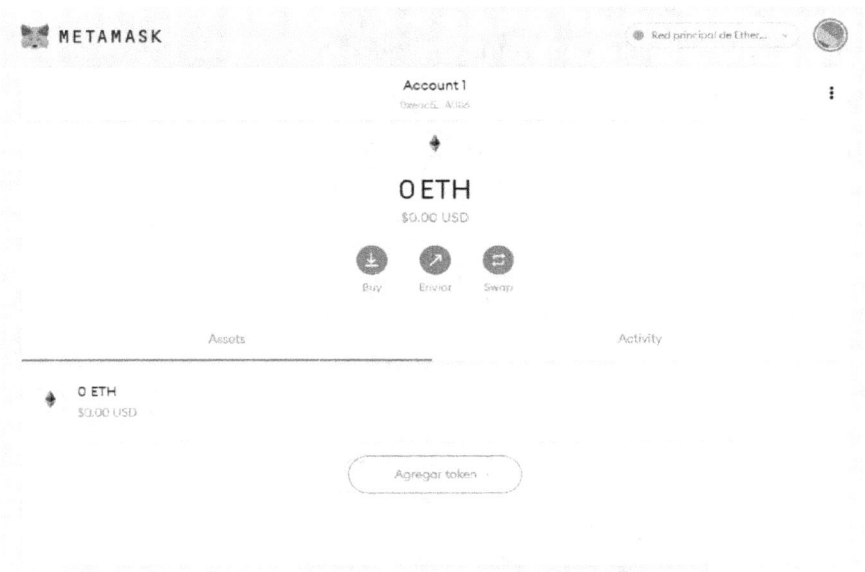

Figure 13.11 MetaMask. Main view

In the upper panel, you will find your wallet's name, Account1 in this case, the amount of cryptocurrency equivalent in ETH and US dollars, and three buttons to buy, send, and exchange crypto, respectively. If you wish to personalize your wallet's name, you only have to click on the three points in a vertical line that appear in the upper right corner. Also, from that same button, you will see all the details of your account at Etherscan and check which sites you are connected to (figure 13.12).

Figure 13.12 MetaMask. Menu

From the account detail, you can modify your wallet's name. In this case, it will be changed to B&C (from Blockchain and cryptocoins). You can also check the details in Etherscan and export your private key (figure 12.13). Remember that you should never, under any circumstances, share your private key with anyone. It would put at risk all the funds you have in your wallet.

Figure 13.13 MetaMask. Details

From the Etherscan window, you can see, in addition to information about your account, your executed or pending transactions status (figure 13.14).

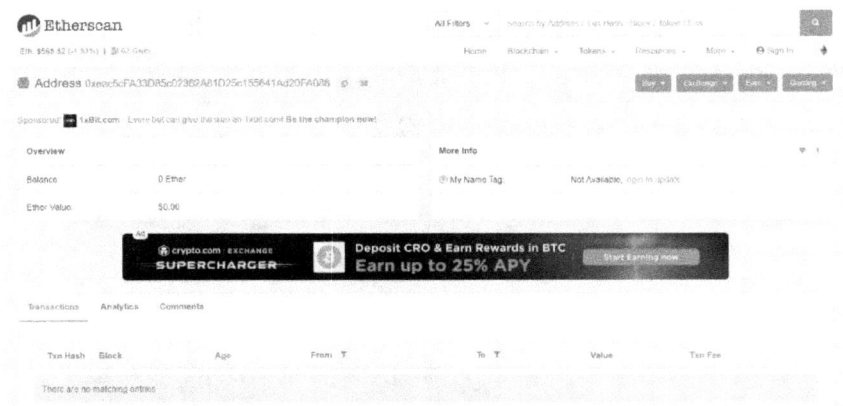

Figure 13.14 Etherscan

Once you have customized your wallet's name, you must add the tokens you wish to store. MetaMask is ready to select from a drop-down list most of the most important ERC20 tokens, but since GEO is still a startup project and is not among the first currencies in ETH, it must be added manually. To do this, click on "Add Token" in the lower panel. Once there, click on the "Custom Token" tab (figure 13.15). The GEO contract number, or the one you wish to add, will be provided by the token's issuing company. In this case, the contract address is

0x147faF8De9d8D8DAAE129B187F0D02D819126750.

You must copy and paste that hexadecimal address into the box called "Token Contract Address." The token name (GEO) and the precision decimals (18) will be set automatically. After

Figure 13.15 MetaMask. Add token

clicking "Next," you will have your wallet configured.

Your wallet should look similar to that shown in figure 13.16.

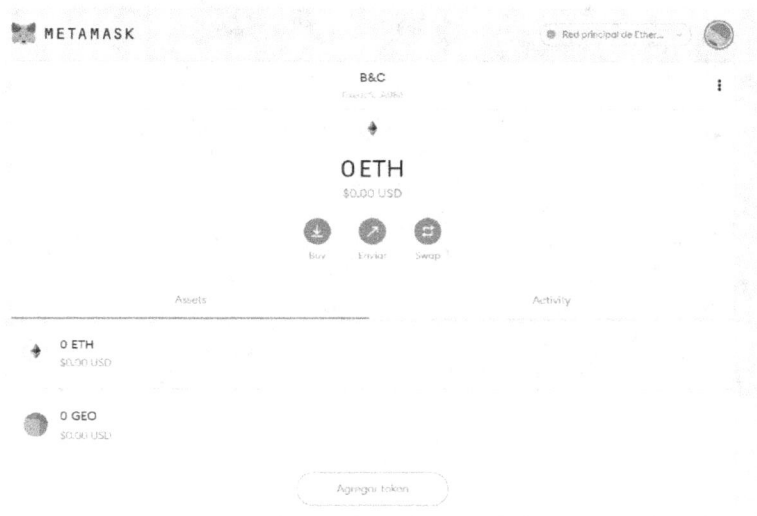

Figure 13.16 MetaMask. Configured wallet

The next step will be to send ETH from the wallet you created in the exchange to your MetaMask wallet (previous example). Click on the name (B&C), which will cause the address to be copied to the clipboard. Log into your Binance account (or the exchange you have chosen) and make the transfer. Once you are in your wallet (you can check the transaction's status on Etherscan), you will have everything you need to make your first crypto to crypto exchange.

Go to the Uniswap page provided by the issuer; for the ETH-GEO/GEO-ETH swap, it is as follows:

https://info.uniswap.org/pair/0xd10122ef86ae040efee3f53f35d324
7230ca670c (figure 13.17).

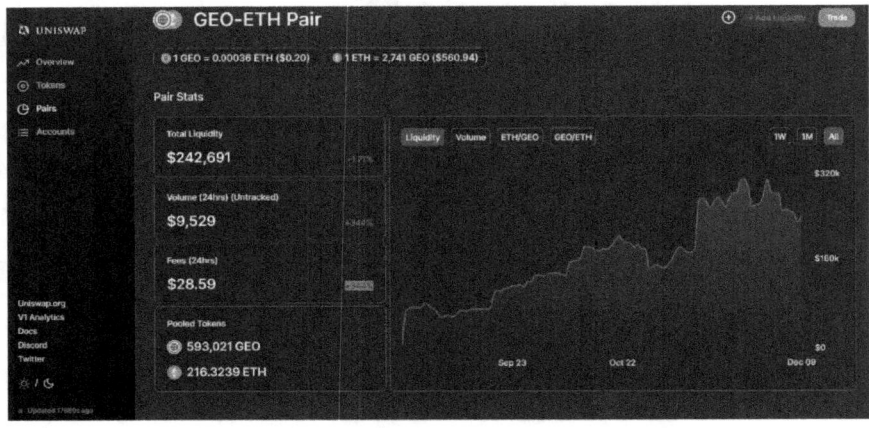

Figure 13.17 Uniswap. GEO-ETH Pair

Click on the "Trading" button in the upper right corner. A new tab will appear where you can perform the swap. Select ETH to GEO (figure 13.18) and click "Swap." Always have a few dollars (in ETH) reserved for gas payment. After completing the transaction, you will find the newly acquired GEOs in your MetaMask wallet. In the next paragraph, you will find the instructions to participate with your GEOs on a yield-farming mechanism.

Figure 13.18 Uniswap. GEO purchase

YIELD FARMING

This concept would include staking and liquidity mining. Through these mechanisms, an investor deposits its tokens in a smart contract or pool and, in return, receives some tokens. A liquidity pool is a smart contract where investors contribute tokens to obtain a return in exchange. The funds are used to create the liquidity necessary for other investors to buy and sell that asset. The return is given by the fees of buying and selling and by the interest earned from lending those tokens. However, through staking, we participate in the block validation in blockchains that use PoS. The profitability is obtained from the compensation that the nodes receive for carrying them out. Besides, in staking, there may be a blocking period during which tokens cannot be removed. In that case, the profitability is usually higher.

Of the most profitable liquidity mining mechanisms in which I have participated, now are those launched by GeoDB. Since it will be possible to participate in new GEO liquidity pools in the future, I will use one example. That will make it easier for you to contribute funds if you wish to do so. It isn't a complicated process, but it may be an unintuitive process for an uninitiated investor.

The first GEO liquidity incentive was available from August to October 2020 and had a maximum participation duration of 90 days, offering an APY of up to 1,200%. Distribution tokens were granted to all those who invested their claim rights on the underlying tokens (a Uniswap-GEO pair, called UNISWAP-V2-GEO-ETH2) in a smart contract called TokenGeyser.

TokenGeyser distributes rewards based on the amount invested, investment time, and an incentive bonus for long-term participation. This bonus is a multiplier over the participation in the distribution token geyser that starts at one and increases linearly over time until 60 days, when the bonus reaches a multiplier of 3.

Since you learned how to exchange ETH for GEO in the previous section, this example will start from that very moment.

To participate in this DeFi product, as with all Uniswap yield farming, you must contribute the same amount in euros (or dollars) from each of the two pairs of participating currencies. Thus, in this case, $100 will be invested in ETH and the same GEO amount.

First, add the address of the new token to your MetaMask wallet (0x7b1be7f8e6431514b20029cb7f2242ff9081b4b2 in this case). Then go to the website where the token issuer allows you to purchase Uniswap tokens. This case is the same as seen in the previous example (figure 13.17), but this time clicks on "Add

Figure 13.19 Uniswap. Add liquidity

Liquidity." You will then access a website very similar to the one you used to buy GEO, but this time dedicated to purchasing a new token, the UNISWAP-V2-GEO-ETH2, which will be exchanged for the $200 in GEOs and ETHs mentioned above (figure 13.19).

Plug in your MetaMask wallet and enter the corresponding amounts and remember to leave a few dollars in the wallet for the gas payment. Confirm the operation and check that the tokens have been charged to your wallet.

So far, this would be the normal process of providing liquidity in Uniswap. In this case, besides, the tokens of the UNISWAP-V2-GEO-ETH2 pair will be deposited in the GeoDB geyser to obtain additional profitability. To do so, connect your wallet to the liquidity pool provided by the issuer, https://geoliquidity.geodb.com/, for the case of GEO (figure 13.20).

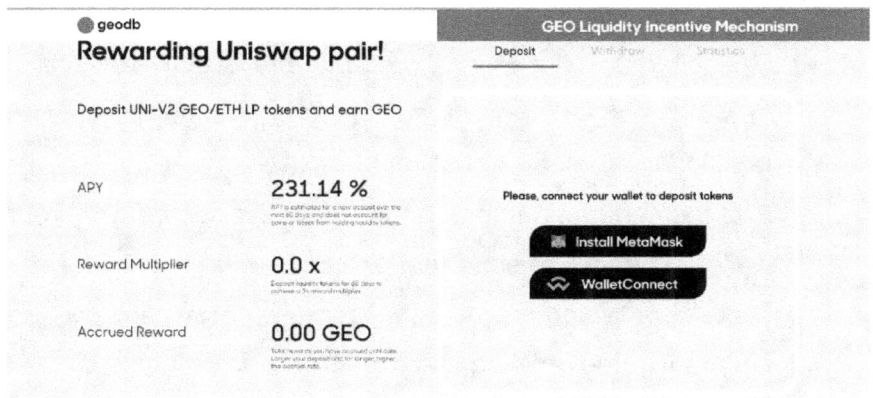

Figure 13.20 Geoliquidity

Connect your MetaMask wallet, deposit your UNISWAP-V2-GEO-ETH2 tokens and confirm the operation. From that moment on, you will be able to access the platform periodically to see how your profits increase day by day.

If you wish to withdraw the funds at any time, you should go to the "Withdraw" tab, withdraw the UNISWAP-V2-GEO-ETH2 tokens, and the reward in the form of a GEO. The Uniswap tokens should be exchanged for your original ETHs and GEOs on the Uniswap website provided by the issuer.

ICOs

Participating in an ICO is a relatively simple process. First, you must access the platform indicated by the project in which you want to invest. It can be an exchange or simply their website. Usually, the company's tokens are exchanged for ETH so that the process would be similar to the following:

- Deposit in a wallet of your property, preferably TrustWallet or MetaMask, the amount of ETH to be transferred plus an additional $20 or $30 to cover gas costs.
- Add the contract address provided by the company to your wallet to be able to store the tokens.
- Make the shipment to the address provided by the company after verifying that it is correct.
- Check that the transaction has been carried out correctly and that you have received the expected amount of tokens.

Keep in mind that around ICOs, there are countless attempts at fraud. You must check that the company's website or platform where the address to send the tokens is indicated real. On multiple occasions, hackers have created similar pages with different addresses to steal the tokens destined for the ICO.

The variety of DeFi operations that can be performed is much greater, but they are not the book's subject, as they involve advanced knowledge and high risk. In any case, those described here are the main ones in which you can participate.

Remember the main point of this chapter:

> Different types of wallets can be used for different purposes.
>
> For large volumes of currencies, the best solution would be to opt for a hardware wallet, while for day-to-day operations, it would be best to use a mobile/web wallet such as TrustWallet MetaMask.
>
> Please note that:
> - You should only invest a small percentage of the equity portion of your portfolio.
> - Depending on your risk profile, the equity portion should be between 10-15% and 80% of the total.
> - Do not invest money that you may need in the short or medium term. The volatility of cryptoassets is very high.
> - Invest only in those products you know. Spend the necessary time studying what you are planning to invest in.
>
> Exchanges between fiat money and cryptocurrencies can only be done in centralized exchanges. However, crypto/crypto can also be done in decentralized ones, much cheaper and safer.
>
> One of the most profitable DeFi mechanisms is yield farming, whereby an investor deposits his tokens in a smart contract or pool and, in return, receives some tokens.
>
> Participating in an ICO is very simple. In most cases, it is enough to exchange the tokens with ETH.

> Keep in mind that ICOs are very high-risk operations (with which very high revaluations can be obtained) and that, in some cases, they can be scams.

Chapter 14: Taxation

"Government's view of the economy could be summed up in a few short phrases: If it moves, tax it. If it keeps moving, regulate it. And if it stops moving, subsidize it."

Ronald Reagan, USA ex-president

It had to get here. Sooner or later, politicians had to confiscate their piece of cake. It's their modus vivendi. It was to be expected. There have been pressures in the European Union, mostly from Spain, to increase the cryptocurrency-related activities regulation. Within this attempt to stem the tide, some positive measures such as the legal framework needed to launch an ICO. If they do not present a white paper, the authorities can warn of the possibility of fraud. That is nothing more than a paternalistic measure. The minimum that any common-sense investor should do is study it together with the business model, the reputation and history of the company, and its income and expenditure forecasts.

In reality, the currencies most affected by future European legislation will be the stablecoins, whose issuers will have to apply for a license and reflect their support mechanisms in a technical document.

As for the tax issue, there are indeed more significant discrepancies between governments, and here the main differences will be broken down.

Spain

Since this is my home country, I will start with Spain, where the government wants to address tax legislation as soon as possible to, literally, *"clean up the crypto-currencies' image."* The phrase qualifies itself so that I will go directly to detail the state of the legislation.

In Spain, financial operations are those cryptocurrencies that have been used as a means of payment by all parties involved in a transaction. Thus, they are exempt from the payment of VAT, as they are not considered as goods or services. As you can guess, it leaves a very important legal vacuum since the greatest projection of blockchains will come from tokenization.

In summary, cryptoassets have the same fiscal categorization as stocks, so the results of operations on them will be framed within the heading of profits and losses in the tax return. Thus, the tax rates for the profits obtained through the sale of cryptocurrencies will be:

- 19% for earnings under 6,000 euros.
- 21% for earnings between 6,000 and 50,000 euros.
- 23% for earnings over 50,000 euros.

These rates also apply to profits earned, even if the currencies have not been withdrawn from the wallet or exchanged for fiat money. In any case, at present, it is almost impossible to identify the cryptographic wallets' owners, so they are still pies in the air.

As far as mining is concerned, the equivalent in euros of all the currencies obtained would have to be incorporated into the tax base of the tax year in question, thus applying the corresponding income tax to their earnings.

Germany

It is now time to analyze my country of residence. Unlike what happens in Spain, they are not considered as stocks or commodities, but cryptocurrencies are considered as private money. That is important because according to the EStG law, the first 600 euros are tax-free, but no charge will be paid if the cryptoassets are kept more than one year in the portfolio. It is not surprising that the Teutonic country is becoming a superpower in the crypto world since they also follow strategies that aim to stimulate innovation in blockchains by allowing the free market. In 2013, the BaFin (Bundesanstalt für Finanzdienstleistungsaufsicht) published a guide that considered certain tokens as alternatives to legal tender. The new legislation being prepared focuses on the regulation of ICOs, similar to what is being considered in the EU, and the modification of bureaucratic rules to facilitate the registration of securities, to reduce the time and cost of procedures.

But that's not all. The most important bank in Germany, Deutsche Bank, is convinced that cryptocurrencies will replace cash in the future and is preparing for it. Specifically, they are betting on a CBDC (Central Bank Digital Currency), issued by the European Central Bank.

USA

As in Spain, in the United States, cryptocurrencies are not considered currency, but as a property, like shares or a house. Therefore, the result of cryptoasset operations will be included in the capital gains and losses section as long as they fall into one of these two categories:

- Exchange of cryptocoin for fiat money or another cryptocoin.
- Use of cryptocoin for the sale of goods and services.
- Interest received for investment in DeFi products except staking.

As in Germany, there is a differentiation between capital gains for investments that exceed the year and those that do not. According to the IRS's assumptions, the following table includes the different tax brackets (Internal Revenue Service).

Investment of less than a year			
Rate	Single/indv. declaration	Married with joint declaration	Householders
10%	$0 < income <= $9,875	$0 < income <= $19,750	$0 < income <= $14,100
12%	$9,875 < income <= $40,125	$19,750 < income <= $80,250	$14,100 < income <= $53,700
22%	$40,125 < income <= $85,525	$80,250 < income <= $171,050	$53,700 < income <= $85,500
24%	$85,525 < income <= $163,300	$171,050 < income <= $326,600	$85,500 < income <= $163,300
32%	$163,300 < income <= $207,350	$326,600 < income <= $414,700	$163,300 < income <= $207,350
35%	$207,350 < income <= $518,400	$414,700 < income <= $622,050	$207,350 < income <= $518,400
37%	income > $518,400	income > $622,050	income > $518,400
Investment of more than a year			
0%	$0 < income <= $40,000	$0 < income <= $80,000	$0 < income <= $53,600
15%	$40,000 < income <= $441,450	$80,000 < income <= $496,600	$53,600 < income <= $469,050
20%	income > $441,450	income > $496,600	income > $469,050

The above cases therefore exclude from taxation the exchange of fiat money for cryptocurrencies and donations. In such cases, taxes will only be paid after the sale of the cryptocoins are received.

Mining and staking are included in the income category as self-employed, with a tax burden of 15.3% as long as more than $400 is mined. Mining expenses such as purchase or rental of HW, electricity, and depreciation suffered by the HW itself can be deducted.

Rewards received through airdrops are considered ordinary income.

In any case, the assumptions mentioned here may change at any time due to regulatory changes, so they should be considered only as a guide, having to confirm with the tax authority of your country of residence what are the tax rates and the correct way to make the corresponding tax return.

Remember the main points of this chapter:

> There are many differences in tax matters between countries, although, in most of them, operations with cryptocurrencies fall within the category of capital gains and losses.
>
> Please note that the data provided in this chapter is offered as a guide, and it is you who must ensure that you comply with the tax legislation of your country of residence.

Chapter 15: Scams

"Impostors do not need to study much the natural causes, but it is enough for them to make use of the common ignorance, stupidity, and superstition of humanity."

Thomas Hobbes, philosopher

The inclusion of this chapter at the end of this book is not accidental. For a while, I was in doubt about the appropriateness of presenting it in the last position instead of interspersing it between sections. The truth is that the risk of leaving the reader with a bad taste in his mouth is high, but the principle of prudence advised me that a disbeliever is better than a convinced swindler. That is why I think it is only fair to show the crypto world's less friendly face as a warning by a colophon.

During 2020, more than 30 million US dollars were swindled through scams related to cryptocurrencies. It's an amazing amount, but even more so are the most common types of scams. I assume that the reader of this book would not fall for the scams mentioned here because the mere fact of buying and reading this type of book reflects a certain cultural and intellectual level. In any case, I am obliged to detail the most common scams and how to avoid them.

The first principle to follow, not only in the crypto world but in any area of life, is that "if you pay peanuts, you get monkeys." Even so, Ponzi schemes and pyramid schemes are still the order of the day. A clear example is the advertisements that promise to double or even triple the amount of tokens or coins deposited in the supposed investment. It is very popular among Facebook groups related to cryptocurrencies.

Another of the most delirious forms of fraud is the impersonation of a famous person or company, such as that which occurred on a YouTube channel posing as Elon Musk, asking people to send BTC to a wallet address with the promise of a full refund plus some benefits.

It's also very common in recent times for social networks such as Facebook or Telegram to offer free tokens in the form of "giveaways" or "airdrops" (watch out, many are real and are used to promote new tokens) accessed through a fraudulent website. It asks for a certain amount of cryptocurrency or your bank details so that it can do the job for you. Keep in mind that real giveaways or airdrops will never ask you for personal data except for a virtual wallet address.

The last of that kind of foolish fraud is when a scammer asks someone to make a P2P exchange of a cryptocurrency at a ridiculous price. Once he receives the funds, he disappears with the money.

Up to this point, the scams that no one with common sense should fall into. However, there are indeed a series of more elaborate frauds in which you should pay attention not to fall into the scammers' traps. The most common causes are the following:

Fake ICOs

When robbers create a false project and request financing through a token sale at a low price, they disappear, and the investors lose all their money once the tokens are sold.

Cloud mining fake companies

Chapter five mentioned that many of the companies supposedly engaged in cloud mining are fake. It is estimated that by the end of 2020, the number of fraudulent companies exceeded 80%. They are easily identifiable because they offer a much higher return than real companies like Genesis or CCG.

Pump & dump schemes

It is not only a cryptoasset scam. It is also produced with stock shares. It is based on inflating an asset's price through massive purchases obtained with fraudulent marketing that includes false information. When the price reaches the level the fraudster desires, the tokens or shares are sold by him, who pockets large profits while the asset's price falls abruptly with no signs of recovery.

In summary, before participating in any operation that involves a disbursement of money, consider the following tips:

- Study the product, spend enough time getting to know the project or asset you want to invest in.
- Be wary of gifts if you are asked for personal data or crypto money in return.
- Buy cryptoassets through recognized exchanges and never through P2P transactions with individuals you do not know.
- Never share your wallet's private key.
- Do not trust investments that promise very high returns if they do not come from a serious company.

I am sure that with these simple tips, you will never have to regret having participated in a fraudulent investment.

Remember the main points of this chapter:

> The vast majority of scams that occur in the crypto world are easily avoidable.
>
> The first maxim to follow, not only in the crypto world but in any area of life, is that "if you pay peanuts, you get monkeys."
>
> There are more elaborate scams, so extreme caution should be exercised in certain operations. Fake ICO and cloud mining companies are examples of that.
>
> Keep in mind the following tips:
> - Study the product, spend enough time getting to know the project or asset you want to invest in and its managers.
> - Be wary of gifts if you are asked for personal data or cryptocurrency in exchange.
> - Buy cryptoassets through recognized exchanges and never through P2P transactions with individuals you do not know.
> - Never share the private key of your wallet.
> - Do not trust investments that promise very high returns if they do not originate from a recognized company.

Conclusions

"Blockchain is the biggest opportunity set we can think of over the next decade or so."

Bob Greifeld, Nasdaq Chief Executive

By the end of 2018, it was estimated that the total amount of money in the world was around 106 billion dollars, counting deposits and current accounts. The total amount of gold was 9 trillion, and the stock market assets 80. The total debt amounted to 200 billion dollars.

During the crisis caused by the COVID-19, the central banks increased their debt purchase programs in support of the big banks and companies. The EU granted loans to its member states, whose destiny, controlled by the local governments, was none other than increasing the number of votes and not so much to improve the productive system. As in all crises, the citizen was impoverished by new debt issues so that a certain ruling class sees its interests protected. The result is that the debt generated is unpayable. A large part of the already existing debt will fall into speculative level ratings and make issuing new debt more expensive. A default scenario in several countries is not unreasonable. It has already happened in countries like Argentina more than once.

Unfortunately, the current system is unsustainable. That's why since the 2008 crisis, a new alternative has emerged that has grown rapidly in recent years: Bitcoin. Little by little, it has become the gold 2.0 even though it is an unconsolidated financial technology. What is the reason why people are launching to invest in bitcoin in particular or Blockchain in general? Without a doubt, the blockchain has meant a technological disruption equivalent to that caused by the Internet's generalization or the Industrial Revolution.

Nobody could imagine the new business models and the new professions that the Internet's arrival would bring to the homes. Google, Amazon, Facebook, among others, changed the way we see the world. Something similar will happen in the very near future with Blockchain technologies. Still, with a fundamental difference: Only a few privileged people had the opportunity to jump on the bandwagon of new technologies in the '90s. However, at this time, anyone can be a participant in this new revolution that, little by little, will change the world.

DAO and tokenization are two concepts that will democratize the economy in a way never seen before. Accessing these products is much easier than doing so with any financial instrument and much lower cost.

Blockchains bring advantages such as robustness to attacks, greater tolerance to failures, traceability and immutability taken to the extreme, and democratization of decision-making.

At the dawn of a new political system, we are still far from being consolidated, but cryptocracy is an unstoppable phenomenon. It represents the most significant potential redistribution of wealth that could ever be imagined.

You have the opportunity to participate in it at the beginning of its creation. Not only in bitcoin, whose value has multiplied by more than 600,000 since its creation and could still be revalued by 50 in the coming years, but with the rest of cryptoassets and technologies related to blockchains.

Being a DAO shareholder is as simple as buying the tokens that the company issues for this purpose. This way, you can participate in an automatically managed company, with public and transparent rules where token holders will decide how and when to change the automatic rules if they wish to do so.

All those businesses related to supply chains will be significantly affected positively because blockchains' adoption will mean a very high reliability and cost reduction. The bureaucracy of the activities related to the transfer of goods will be immediate and much cheaper. It will not be necessary to go to the registry office to buy a house. All this will be registered in a blockchain at an almost ridiculous cost.

There will be no room for corruption because all the funds will be traced, and there will be no possibility of hiding a transaction or modifying it.

Thanks to the DeFi, the need for a reliable third party to certify transactions are eliminated, costs have been reduced, profitability has increased, and the offer of new financial products has multiplied, extending it to a public with difficult access to this type of product. From your cell phone, you could participate in the purchase of tokens that give you the right to share in the profits of a solar farm in China, finance a dam in Zimbabwe, or receive part of the rental income from an apartment in New York.

The importance of the DeFi is such that the real scope they could achieve and all the products they can offer is not yet known. Economists agree that they are here to stay and will increasingly gain market share and force a change in the current way of investing, managing, and understanding finance worldwide.

As Christine Lagarde has said, *"Distributed registration technologies such as cryptocurrency and digital assets are shaking up the system."*

You are only one step away from being part of this revolution. It's up to you to be part of it or not. Take your computer, open your first wallet and transfer to it your first cryptocurrencies or fractions of them. As in the analog world, only invest what you don't need in the long run. Research companies and study products. The dead coins cemetery is immense, but that does not mean that those who have survived (or those yet to arrive) are not in good health.

It is the first time that the average citizen is aware that he can be part of the future and the entry barriers are not high. It is a unique opportunity in history. It is up to you to take advantage of it.

Acronyms Glossary

AAVE	AAVE token
ADA	Cardano token
AE	Aeternity token
ARS	Argentinian Peso
ASIC	Application-Specific Integrated Circuit
ATOM	Cosmos token
BaFin	Bundesanstalt für Finanzdienstleistungsaufsicht
BAT	Basic Attention Token
BCH	Bitcoin Cash
BCN	Bytecoin
BCS	Bitcoin Diamond
BitARS	BitShares
BLK	Blackcoin
BNB	Binance Coin
BTC	Bitcoin
BTG	Bitcoin Gold
BSV	Bitcoin SV
CBDC	Central Bank Digital Currency
CEL	Celsius token

CEO	Chief Executive Officer
CPU	Central Processing Unit
CRO	Cryptocoin token
DAI	Dai token
DAO	Decentralized Autonomous Organization
DApp	Decentralized Application
DASC	Dascoin token
DASH	Dash token
DCR	Decred token
DeFi	Decentralized Finance
DLT	Distributed Ledger Technology
DOGE	Dogecoin token
DOT	Polkadot token
dPoS	Delegated Proof of Stake
ECB	European Central Bank
EEA	Enterprise Ethereum Alliance
EOA	Externally Owned Account
EOS	EOS token
ETC	Ethereum Classic
ETH	Ether/Ethereum

ETN	Electroneum token
EVM	Ethereum Virtual Machine
FCA	Financial Conduct Authority
FCT	Firmachain token
FDR	Firma Data Reward
FPGA	Field Programmable Gate Array
GB	Gigabyte
HT	Huobi token
HW	Hardware
ICO	Initial Coin Offering
ICX	ICON token
IRS	Internal Revenue Service
KYC	Know Your Customer
KWh	Kilowatt/hour
LINK	Chainlink token
LPoS	Leased Proof of Stake
LSK	Lisk token
LTC	Litecoin
MB	Megabyte
MBA	Master of Business Administration

ODIN	Open Data Interoperable Network
OKB	OKB token
OMG	OMG token
P2P	Peer to Peer
PoS	Proof of Stake
PoET	Proof of Elapsed Time
PoI	Proof of Importance
PPLNS	Pay Per Last N Shares
PPS	Pay Per Share
PoW	Proof of Work
REP	Augur token
RPoW	Reusable Proof of Work
SDK	Software Development Kit
SEC	U.S. Securities and Exchange Commission
SPV	Simple Payment Verification
SW	Software
TH	TeraHash
TH/s	Terahash/second
TRX	TRON token
UE	Unión Europea
UK	United Kingdom

UNI	Uniswap token
USA	United States of America
USD	American Dollar
USDC	USD Coin token
USDT	Tether token
VAT	Value Added Tax
VET	VeChain token
VHDL	Very High-Speed Integrated Circuit Hardware Description Language
WAN	WanChain token
WAVE	Wave token
wBTC	Wrapped Bitcoin token
WoW	World of Warcraft
XEM	NEM token
XLM	Stellar token
XMR	Monero token
XRP	Ripple token
XTZ	Tezos token
YFI	Yearn.finance token
ZEC	Zcash token

ZRX 0x token

Figure index

Figure I.1	Children are playing with Deutsche Marks during hyperinflation. Source: rarehistoricalphotos.com
Figure 1.1	Network typologies
Figure 1.2	Whitfield Diffie and Martin Hellman. Source: Wikipedia
Figure 2.1	David Chaum. Source: Wikipedia
Figure 2.2	Adam Back's Twitter profile
Figure 3.1	Node distribution in a blockchain
Figure 6.1	Vitálik Buterin. Source: Wikipedia
Figure 7.1	Transactions inside the Ethereum network
Figure 12.1	AAVE. Deposits
Figure 12.2	AAVE. Loans
Figure 13.1	Binance Buy crypto
Figure 13.2	Binance. Crypto purchase with credit card
Figure 13.3	Binance. Trading platform
Figure 13.4	Binance. Trading platform configuration
Figure 13.5	Binance. MA configuration
Figure 13.6	Binance. MA crossing
Figure 13.7	MetaMask. Installation

Figure 13.8   MetaMask. Add extension

Figure 13.9   MetaMask. Password

Figure 13.10   MetaMask. Secret backup phrase

Figure 13.11   MetaMask. Main view

Figure 13.12   MetaMask. Menu

Figure 13.13   MetaMask. Details

Figure 13.14   Etherscan

Figure 13.15   MetaMask. Add token

Figure 13.16   MetaMask. Configured wallet

Figure 13.17   Uniswap. GEO-ETH pair

Figure 13.18   Uniswap. GEO purchase with ETH

Figure 13.19   Uniswap. Add liquidity

Figure 13.20   Geoliquidity

Acknowledgments

To my two daughters, the lights that erase the shadows that try to darken my daily life.

About the author

Born in Malaga in 1981, Antonio Luis Lara has been a computer consultant for more than 15 years. He is a telecommunications engineer from the University of Malaga. He has an MBA from the Chamber of Commerce of Malaga, with prestigious professors such as D. Ramon Tamames or D. Mario Weitz, in which he obtained one of the best grades of his promotion.

He has worked for multinationals such as Mapfre, CSC, Accenture, Bayer, SEAT, Banco Sabadell, and Suez. He currently works in Luxembourg as an external consultant for the European Commission. He collaborates with GeoDB as an ambassador for the company.

www.ingramcontent.com/pod-product-compliance
Lightning Source LLC
Chambersburg PA
CBHW070628220526
45466CB00001B/124